| DATE DUE | | | |
|---|---|---|---|
| | | | |
| | | | |
| | | | |
| | | | |
| | | | |
| | | | |
| | | | |
| | | | |
| | | | |
| | | | |
| | | | |
| | | | |
| | | | |
| | | | |

# MONTANA'S
# MISSOURI RIVER

Number Eight

by R. C. Gildart

PUBLISHED BY

## Montana Magazine, Inc.

HELENA, MONTANA 59604

RICK GRAETZ, PUBLISHER
MARK THOMPSON, PUBLICATIONS DIRECTOR
CAROLYN CUNNINGHAM, EDITOR

This series intends to fill the need for in-depth information about Montana subjects. The concept behind the geographic books is to explore the historical color, the huge landscape and the resilient people of a single Montana subject area. Design and layout production completed in Helena, Montana. Typesetting by Falcon Press, Helena, Montana. Color lithography–DNP America, San Francisco. Printed in Japan.

Total eclipse of the sun from Fred
Robinson Bridge, February, 1979. Ron McCoy.

Montana Magazine, Inc.
Box 5630, Helena, MT 59604
ISBN 0-938314-10-6

**Acknowledgements:**
The author gratefully acknowledges
help provided by Dave Walter of
the Montana Historical Society;
Marge Foote, librarian of the Great
Falls Tribune; Charles M. Russell
Refuge Manager Ralph Fries; pilot
Rich Johnson; Janet Allen; floating
companions David Gildart, nephew
Joel Wright, and Robert C. Gildart
Sr. A last note of thanks to my
parents who invariably provide
comments that enhance my work.

# Contents

Top: Tom Wilson; one of the rugged and individualistic ranchers operating on the Charles M. Russell Refuge.

Bottom: Caspian tern. Robert Gildart.

**About The Author:**
R. C. "Bert" Gildart is a writer/photographer whose work has appeared in National Geographic, Smithsonian, International Wildlife, Sierra Club Books and Living Wilderness. He is the principal author of Montana Wildlife and co-author of Glacier Country, two books in the Montana Geographic Series.

# Introduction

*November ice laps at gunnels. Robert Gildart*

On a warm clear autumn day near Virgelle, Montana, several companions and I pushed canoes into the cold and murky waters of the Missouri River. Although frost had formed the previous night, and leaves from cottonwood trees that line the river's banks had long since scattered and been shifted by autumn winds, winter seemed light years away. As if to punctuate our sense of euphoria, a pheasant cackled from a nearby pile of rose-colored brush while overhead a gaggle of geese soared. There was no sense of urgency in their motions as they glided on, choosing a downriver course, honking among themselves. We watched as they skidded to a stop along water that reflected hardly a ripple from the lavender glow of a gorgeous day.

Frequently, during our five-day sojourn, we stopped and hunted for geese, pheasant or deer, returning early each night to camp beneath a universe full of stars. This day was no exception, and we kindled a fire to take away the chill and recounted the day's events—Tom had shot a deer, Dave a pheasant, I pictures.

Sometime after midnight a breeze began to stir the folds of our tent. As the night progressed the breeze became a full-scale wind. No longer were the folds flapping, rather the entire tent began to moan. We nestled deeper into our down-filled bags.

At dawn, we awoke to an entirely different setting. The wind had completely subsided, but the air was cold—five above according to Dave's pocket thermometer—and now our world was the color of ash. Even the outsides of our sleeping bags were covered with a layer of white—formed as the moisture from our bodies had contacted the frigid air.

During the night, a thin skin of ice had formed along the banks. Having struck camp and loaded our canoes, we soon pushed off. A crackle of ice broke the hushed world, and small flakes of snow were falling. But the temperature remained steady. We had 20 miles to paddle.

This arctic environment was unlike any I'd experienced before. The current was slower; ice was beginning to form. It congealed on our paddles. It gathered in fine layers along the sides of our aluminum canoes. It edged gradually outward from the banks, extending toward the swiftest portion of the river. No pheasants cackled and no geese soared. Along the banks the rock obelisks, columns, and table top formations that stood out boldly against variegated skies were now framed in a layer of white.

What a place to dwell on the West. What a place for the imagination to run—this huge sprawling river that begins in Montana with snowmelt from countless winter streams.

But the cold Missouri has a way of quickly bringing one back from the romantic to the present. Now, the temperature was dropping. It was too cold for rain to fall. Too cold, also, for the falling snow to melt and penetrate our heavy down parkas. The frigid Missouri seemed a desperately lonesome and silent place.

But change in scenery, color, and weather are one of the many lures of the Missouri. In a matter of only 24 hours, the countryside can range from sublime to fickle and capricious. Hundreds of artists have been lured here to capture her quiet beauties on canvas. This is an area where wind, snow, and ice have always played a major part in revealing the heroism of those who plied the river's currents or settled along her banks.

Weather was a major concern for the steamboat Gray Eagle of the late 1800's, which was cut loose by ice from her moorings and sank near Poplar, Montana.

It was a major concern for residents of towns such as Fort Benton and Great Falls when ice jams once forced water along their streets.

But on this particular arctic day, the river was becoming an area of vast intrigue for us. We were unmolested and carefree, not another soul could be seen. And so we paddled on, each gathering in his own thoughts and memories. As we drifted by historic landmarks now etched with snow, we realized that the Missouri is still one of America's most majestic and remote rivers, a fact that should never be altered in our lifetime.

In its natural state, the Missouri once carried 120 tons of mud suspended in each million gallons of water. Steamboats were forced to stop often to clean the mud from their boilers. Early-day homesteaders would take a bucket of river water and let the mud settle to the bottom; then the clear water on top was very good to drink. They said the Missouri was "too thick to drink, to thin to plow."

Since that time, people have built towns along its banks, impounded its once turbulent forces, and changed its course. But the Missouri still

*Although most people think first of Montana's mountains as home of the state's famous game animals, the shores of the Missouri are a wildlife haven. Left: Pheasant. Alan Carey. Right: Mule deer. Tom Ulrich.*

dominates even an altered scene—dominates, just as when, on its own, it modified the original landscape by jumping its banks, creating huge glacial lakes, eroding its path, and exposing bizarre forms of life that lived millions of years ago.

This day, in colder clime, and eight hours after first breaking ice, we beached near Judith Landing—cutting through several inches of mush ice along the banks, appreciating the legacy the Missouri has given us and the story she unfolds for the adventurer of today!

5

# Geology

## Time at Work

Time! The Missouri River represents time in a way that few other natural features can. Time that can be recalled and also made to account for itself.

Here in Montana, the river exposes almost 200 million years. In five days, a floater can travel eastward 150 miles from Fort Benton to the Fred Robinson Bridge—through relics of the ancient past to the present—an average of 30 miles and 40 million years a day.

The float starts more than 250 million years ago in a region being visited by a series of successive seas. The seas are transitory, their stability influenced by mountains just then beginning to form. The gradual uplifting movement of the Belt Mountains from within the surrounding waters elevates the sea floor sufficiently to create stretches of low-lying lands and marshes. But, like the sea, the land masses are also transitory. A subsequent, gradual depression of the area permits the sea to encroach once again.

More time. About 136 million years of time. Now the floor of the sea re-emerges to form lowlands pocketed with shallow lakes and swamps. The climate is semitropical and permits luxuriant growths of ferns and rushes.

Geologists call this semi-tropical segment of time the Cretaceous Period. At its zenith it produced a world filled with vegetation similar to today's Everglades of Florida. But the fauna was decidedly different. Along the shores of the sea roamed dinosaurs—huge animals, vicious animals, peaceful animals. Here plodded the ferocious meat eater, Tyrannosarus Rex, and peaceful three-horned vegetarian, Triceratops.

One of the few reminders of this bygone era is the horned lizard. Magnify it 100 times and one begins to realize the size of its huge ancestors. Rather than scurrying through the ancient Ginkos, they scramble through the bunch grass bordering today's Missouri River where, unlike their distant cousins, they are occasionally seen carrying young on their backs. Docile, they slink through their environment, prey to virtually every type of bird that soars overhead. They are an anachronism but, along the Missouri where bones of ancient creatures are frequently discovered, they seem a little less out of time and place.

Fragments of these ancient reptiles are uncovered each year by the actions of the Missouri River. Few other places in North America have proved so fossily fertile. In 1979 a rancher working his range along the breaks of the Missouri north of Jordan discovered a partially exposed

The horned lizard is a diminutive reminder of the days when huge reptiles roamed Missouri River Country. Robert Gildart.

skull and advised Dr. Mick Hager, curator of the Museum of the Rockies in Bozeman of his finding. It was fall, so Hager quickly assembled a crew. They hoped to unearth the huge animal before the ground froze and snow fell. Working virtually day and night they succeeded, and now MORT, or Museum of the Rockies Triceratops, graces the museum's halls. By its presence, Mort tells more of the story about what Montana was like about 60 to 70 million years ago.

According to Dr. Hager, Mort lived on the coastal plains east of the Rockies and filled a similar role in the late Cretaceous Period that the rhinoceros fills in Africa today. The landscape was replete with an amazing diversity of reptiles—big, small, swimming, flying. But, then, they all vanished, and no one really knows why. For more than 170 million years, today's Missouri River country hosted one of the most long-lived group of animals to have ever evolved. By contrast man has been around only several million years in a world that is about 4 billion years old. All that is known for sure is that these animals were dying out just at the dawn of the mammalian era.

Today, the badlands created by the Missouri produce discoveries each year. For paleontologists, the area has been proved one of the most fertile spots for clues to understanding the evolutionary picture. To appreciate the vast findings, visit the smaller museum at Ft. Peck or the Museum of the Rockies in Bozeman, which was established to accommodate the thousands of relics brought in by dam workers during the '30s.

Yet more time, and again the sea encroaches. It settles, establishing itself in the irregular shape of a giant amoeba. And, like an amoeba, it sends out exploratory arms. Then it gradually draws them back. But in its wake are left more deposits, layers of which in a much more recent time have been exposed, broadly shaped, and then delicately formed by the Missouri River with an assist from wind and rain.

Between Fort Benton and the Fred Robinson Bridge can be seen five different types of rock formations that represent the legacy left by these fickle seas. They were deposited sequentially; as a result, those floating the river pass from the old to the "new."

The first of these formations is referred to as the Colorado group of shales, the elements of which were laid by one of the first inland seas.

*The Missouri badlands give up invaluable pieces of the unfolding story of the dinosaur age every year. This is an artist's rendition of an ancient vegetarian, Maiasaura, with its young plodding the Cretacious-age forests. Tinted lithograph by Doug Henderson.*

Top: Erosion by wind, rain, snow and ice on sedimentary rock layers of varying hardness has created bizzare formations, such as here along the White Cliffs area. Lawrence Dodge.

Bottom: Forty river miles below Fort Benton, floaters encounter Eagle Sandstone, which contains the shells of marine fauna deposited millions of years ago.  Robert Gildart.

The materials in these formations are readily recognized by their dark grey shade. This type of rock remains with the floater for about 50 miles. The landscape along this stretch is rather drab, but near Eagle Creek becomes more interesting. Eagle Sandstone is encountered, and forms the beginning of what floaters consider the picturesque area of "White Rocks." The opal-colored materials in this stone were deposited along the shoreline of a shallow marine sea. Embedded in these sedimentary deposits are the remains of marine animals such as mollusks. Many of the area's most spectacular formations have been carved from this relatively soft rock.

Eighty million years later, but only 50 miles or so, floaters encounter the Claggett Shale formation. Layers of this material are as much as 400 feet thick and can again be recognized by their dark greyish appearance. The easily eroded Claggett Shale forms characteristic low, dome-shaped hills with gentle slopes. As with the Eagle Sandstone, fossils of marine life are found in these rocks.

Another 50 million years, near the mouth of the Judith River, begins the Judith River Formation. Sediments from this formation are generally buff in color. Vertebrate remains are found throughout, though known mammal specimens are restricted to the top 50 feet.

The last group of materials to be seen from the river is Bearpaw Shale. These deposits are evidence of the last great advance of an ancient sea into Montana. These rocks are a dark grey and consist of soft shales. Along with the Claggett formation the Bearpaw shales create the syrupy mud that clings to shoes and hold tenaciously to the tires of automobiles. Most call it "gumbo," and it surrounds the Fred Robinson Bridge, 150 miles and 200 million years from Ft. Benton.

## First Tricklings

Following the deposition of these materials and the uplifting of the various mountain ranges, rivers begin to flow. At first they trickle. Then, with the passage of time and change of climate, murky streams begin to coalesce. From these gatherings one massive river eventually emerged, one more powerful and more determined than the others.

Geologists believe the Missouri started its present eastward path about 3 million years ago. As it flowed, the new river encountered the various layers deposited by the seas. In most places the Missouri took the path of least resistance. But one place where it did not detour was at the Gates of the Mountains near Helena. There it flows through the Belt Mountains rather than around them. The Jefferson River does the same thing, passing directly through Jefferson Canyon near the Lewis and Clark Caverns. Why didn't these two rivers choose easier routes?

The Missouri tells the story for both rivers, and the answer reposes in the type of materials they encountered. In the Belt Mountains area, the substance originally blocking the river's path was soft and the Missouri could easily punch its way through and leave in its wake a deep channel. Eventually, the river did encounter materials that were of greater density. When it did, the waters backed up. The growing lakes would search for an outlet so that the river could continue. In the case of the Gates of the Mountains, patience had its reward. The hard rock, the majestic rock we see as we sputter along on the cruise boat Sacajawea, was excised by the Missouri River reaching at long last a spot where there was softer material. Then the impoundment gushed forth, and the river flowed on toward the lower elevations in the east.

## The River Gains Direction

Originally, the Missouri began in the Rockies, cut through the Gates of the Mountains and then flowed rapidly north and east toward Hudson Bay. But there were forces at work that had the power to divert even the Missouri. An infinitesimal number of small, downy, stellar-shaped snowflakes—compacted through the eons into a great mass of glacial ice—forced the waters of this embryonic river toward the Gulf of Mexico.

More time, and eventually the Missouri established a course. It had general direction, but not a fixed channel, for evidence strongly suggests that the Missouri occupied other channels that closely parallel its present one. Today, these channels can be seen in Montana; they provide routes through which other less massive streams can pass.

One of these streams is Sand Coulee Creek which flows south of Great Falls. The stream is

*Top: Agriculture has taken over one of the ancient channels of the Missouri River near Lost Lake. John Reddy.*

*Bottom: Gates of the Mountains. Towering cliffs on each side present a visual study of ancient sea floors. Forms of sea life from 300 million years ago are fossilized and vividly displayed. Lawrence B. Dodge.*

small, and the valley through which it flows is far too large to have been cut by a river as insignificant as Sand Coulee Creek. As further evidence that the valley was created by the Missouri, geologists point out that all tributaries of the creek angle in from the west—just as they would if they were joining an eastward flowing river. And, the Missouri flows east, not west as does Sand Coulee Creek. Apparently, the Missouri once passed to the south of Great Falls.

Another river supporting this conjecture is the Milk River. In many places, it too flows through valleys too large to have been cut by such a relatively small river.

Geologists believe that ice formed from compacted snow, dammed the ancestral Missouri and created an enormous lake that flooded an area extending 10 miles west of Simms, 10 miles south of Cascade, and east as far as the town of Belt. At their maximum, the lake waters reached an elevation of about 3,900 feet.

When the dam ice began to melt, the waters carved a new course, and they did so in a dramatic way. They cut a path through the Highwood Mountains that in places is as much as a mile wide and 500 feet deep. This area is referred to as the Shonkin Sag and is where the towns of Shonkin and Highwood are located today.

## Badlands and Erosion

Regardless of nationality, every explorer passing through the region containing the eastern section of Montana's Missouri River described it in a universal term. To the French they were the Mauvaises Terres;to the English they were called The Badlands.

These badlands are particularly pronounced to the floater riding the current from Eagle Creek to the Fred Robinson Bridge. Between these points, molded by the forces of erosion, one sees oddities such as table-top rocks, castles, monuments and arches. Spectacular to see, their existence represents nature at work for only a few thousand years of the earth's time.

Differential erosion is responsible for many of these forms. Some of the sedimentary layers are softer than others and erode more quickly. Where harder rock covered softer rock, pedestaled, or mushroomed rocks, were created. This type of formation is common throughout the Eagle Sandstone.

*Perhaps another raging Missouri waterfall once gushed over this rocky face at Lost Lake in an old Missouri channel. John Reddy.*

*Table-top rocks, a legacy of erosion through the millenia. Robert Gildart.*

Arches and windows, such as Hole-in-the-Wall and Eye of the Needle, have been carved by similar processes. In this case, softer rock was interspersed in an area of harder rock. Ice, with its incredible force, gradually moved the softer rock. With time, patches of blue sky begin to appear beneath vermillion-colored hard rock. The process is an endless one and, as the Missouri eats away at its banks, new rocks are exposed from beneath a mantle of dirt. Soon, the process of cutting more windows, more arches, begins anew.

Turret-shaped formations, often called castles, have been formed by a slightly different process. When the land was being lifted, the rock in each underground layer was so strained that cracks shot throughout it, and the layer became fractured and crazed like over-fired porcelain. These cracks, called joints, tend to run in surprisingly straight lines. When the rock is exposed to weathering, the joints erode. On cliffs, the process of joint weathering produces large, separated, vertical blocks that eventually are left isolated and free-standing. Steamboat Rock is an example of this type of action.

## Today's River

Today the Missouri is considered to begin at Three Forks, Montana, where it starts its tortuous journey, joining at last with the Mississippi near St. Louis, Missouri. Many writers have expressed the belief that if the Missouri River had been discovered before the Mississippi, the Missouri would have been considered the main stream and the upper Mississippi the tributary. As it meanders from its headwaters west of Yellowstone Park to its junction with the Mississippi, the Missouri travels a distance of 2,546 miles; and to the Gulf of Mexico the Missouri-Mississippi has a length of 4,220 miles.

To further amplify the statistical advantage of the Missouri, it is longer than the entire Mississippi, and more than twice as long as that part of the latter stream above their confluence. It drains a watershed of 580,000 square miles, and the mean total annual discharge is estimated to be 20 cubic miles, or a mean-rate of 94,000 cubic feet per second, which is more than twice the quantity of water discharged by the upper Mississippi.

The Missouri is also the bolder, more rapid, and most turbulent of the two streams. Its muddy water impinges upon the Mississippi. "By every rule of nomenclature," say writers, "the Missouri, being the main stream and the upper Mississippi the tributary, the name of the former should have been given precedence, and the great river—the longest in the world — should have been called 'Missouri' from the Rocky Mountains to the Gulf of Mexico."

In Montana, the river is created by the general confluence of the Madison, Gallatin, and Jefferson rivers at Three Forks. Each of the three headwater rivers is about 90 feet wide, flows with great velocity, and discharges large quantities of water. The Gallatin is the most rapid of the three, but the Jefferson drains the largest area. As Lewis and Clark moved upstream, they treated the Jefferson as a continuation of the Missouri, following it to its source at Lemhi Pass.

Below the junction at Three Forks, the course of the Missouri lies in mountain valleys and deep canyons, finally emerging through a rocky gorge in a range of rocks called by Lewis and Clark the "Gates of the Rocky Mountains." Thirty-five miles above Fort Benton the river pours over a precipice, gives the city of Great Falls its name, and then flows eastwardly.

The area through which the river flows is known as the Missouri River Basin, an agricultural empire of more than half a million square miles. And, though the basin is sparsely populated, in 1975 it produced half of the nation's wheat, a sixth of its pork, a fifth of its beef and butter, and nearly a third of its wool.

As the Missouri makes its cross-country journey it gathers in the water of other rivers. Near Buford, North Dakota, 1600 miles above St. Louis it receives the Yellowstone River. And the Yellowstone—only one of the rivers that make up the Missouri—has three principal tributaries—the Bighorn, the Powder, and the Tongue, whose combined drainage area is slightly larger than the state of Ohio.

But, as one writer so eloquently wrote, "The Missouri is all these and more. It is the Milk and the Musselshell, the Wind and the Sun, the Big Hole and the Beaverhead, the Platte and the James, the Teton and the Fourche, the Niobrara and the Marias, streams of mountains and of plains moving toward their compulsive rendezvous with the distant ocean, carving shadows upon rocks, giving perspective to great spaces almost anesthetic in their dizzying emptiness, reflecting blazing suns and mellow moons, bordering their shores with the tender trees of willows sweet to the eyes of men in a nearly treeless land."

The trip from Montana to St. Louis is a downhill journey. The source of the Missouri lies more than 4,000 feet above sea level. It pours almost 70,000 cubic feet of water into the Mississippi every second. If all this water were to roar straight down the middle of America, its speed would be incredible and destructive.

But nature has a way of slowing down Big Muddy. Its channel twists and turns like a long snake, and each bend helps slow the water and silt of the river. One steamboat traveler counted 173 bends in Montana alone.

One natural reason for all the mud in the Missouri is that its swift current is always carving new channels through the earth. As writer George Fitch put it, "The Missouri is likely to get out of its bed in the middle of the night and hunt up a new one, sweeping trees, brush, even houses before it."

Discovery

Sculptor Bob Scriver provided Fort Benton with his vision of Lewis and Clark and Sacajawea exploring the unknown. Tim Church.

The first white men to explore the Missouri River were greeted with new adventures around every bend. Pere (Father) Jacques Marquette and Father Louis Jolliet were the first Europeans to see the Missouri River. Of this 1673 experience, Marquette wrote, "I have seen nothing more frightful. A mass of large trees enters with branches—real floating islands. They come rushing from the mouth of the Pek-i-tan-oni so impetuously that we cannot without great danger expose ourselves to pass across. Pek-i-tan-oni is a considerable stream which, coming from the northwest, enters the Mississippi."

The next significant explorer to make headway into this mysterious region was another Frenchman. In 1714 Etienne Venyard de Bourgmont traveled up some of the lower Missouri River and became acquainted with the Indians along the way. He met the tribe whose name would later be identified with the river, the Missouri Indians. They were already few in number because many had been killed in a disastrous intertribal war. Before many years had passed, the white man's diseases wiped out the rest—a pattern that was to persist to the Madison, Jefferson, and Gallatin rivers and beyond.

The upper Missouri was explored by Pierre Gaultier, Sieur de La Verendrye, in 1738. He was amazed by the plentiful game and especially the thousands of buffalo.

The first group of men to see the upper Missouri was the Couriers-de-bois. They were French-Canadian trappers, probably half-breeds, and in their habits were blended the innocent simplicity of the fun-loving Frenchman and the wild traits and woodcraft of the Indian. Born in the woods, they were accustomed from childhood to the hardships and exposure of life in the wilderness. Couriers often adopted a tribe's customs and married their women. Each became a "savage."

These progenitors left other descendants both in name and in deed. All along the Missouri, romantic names such as the Marias-des-Cygnes (River of the Swans), Creve-Ceur (Broken Heart), Bonne-Femme (Good Woman), and Terre-Beau (Beautiful Earth), say that here passed a lonely, romantic Frenchman.

Frenchmen also were responsible for the re-establishment of St. Louis. They had been granted the right to trade with the Indians of the Missouri and all nations residing west of the Mississippi River. The city began as a fur trading post or fort in 1764. Yet even as St. Louis was being planned and built, the French secretly had ceded their western lands to Spain. Napoleon retrieved the territory for France in 1801, but by 1803 his plans for colonies in the Western Hemisphere were in deep trouble. A rebellion in Santo Domingo and threatened war with Great Britain persuaded him to sell the Louisiana Territory—800,000 square miles — to the United States for $15 million.

At the time of the sale, no one knew how far the West extended. And no country can govern what it doesn't comprehend. But there was another motive for exploring the new purchase—the old dream of a water route to India and to great wealth.

## Lewis & Clark

Thomas Jefferson knew that a major river called the ''Missouri'' poured into the Mississippi from the west; he also knew that a sea captain named Gray had found a major river emptying into the Pacific and named it the ''Columbia.'' Could it be that their headwaters interlocked? There was no evidence, but some men thought it to be so. They said a crew could take a boat up the Missouri to its source, do a one-day portage, and float down the Columbia to the Pacific. For these reasons, Jefferson had long been interested in sending an expedition into the West. To head the expedition Jefferson choose Meriwether Lewis, his own private secretary. In the army, Lewis had served with distinction, demonstrating leadership and good judgement. Jefferson arranged cram courses for Lewis in navigation, medicine, and natural history.

As a co-leader, Lewis selected William Clark who, like himself, was in his early 30s. Both men were older than the nation. They had been born British citizens before the American Revolution, and Clark's older brother, George Rogers Clark, had played a major role in it. Now they were on a mission of exploration and diplomacy for the young nation.

The captains made final preparations for their exploration in the winter of 1803-4, in St. Louis. Here, they began assembling men and equipment outside the town. By the time the party was

*Lewis and Clark's first glimpses of what is now Montana must have been near this area, which is near the confluence of the Missouri and the*

*Yellowstone Rivers just outside present-day Montana. Jim Romo.*

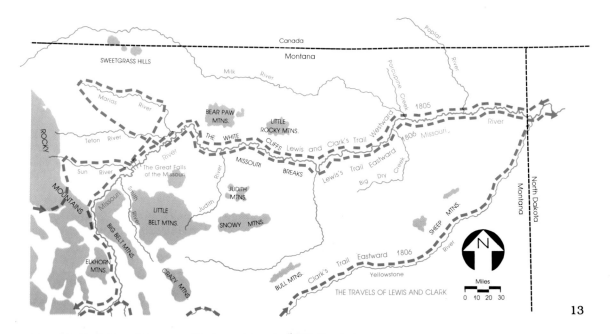

THE TRAVELS OF LEWIS AND CLARK

13

ready to leave, it totaled about 50, most of whom were army men with experience on the frontier. Three boats were loaded for the trip. Two were pirogues, or long, narrow canoes made of hollowed logs and propelled by oars. The other was a 55-foot-long keelboat. This was a flat-bottomed boat especially designed and built for the dangerous, shallow Missouri. It could be rowed with 22 oars, pushed with long poles, towed from the shore, or sailed when the wind was right.

Most of the lower river had been explored before, so the expedition was fairly uneventful for the first few months. But, moving boats upriver against the current was back-breaking work. The men were exhausted after a day of dragging on tow ropes, rowing, and poling. At night they were tormented by fleas, ticks, and huge "musquiters." Then, near Council Bluffs, Sergeant Charles Floyd began to feel ill. His ailment was termed "Biliose Chorlick." He was carried ashore at the present-day site of Sioux City, Iowa, and there died. Sergeant Floyd was the expedition's only fatality despite all the dangers through which it passed. It is generally believed today that Floyd was a victim of a ruptured appendix.

'We buried him on the top of the bluff 1/2 mile below a small river to which we gave his name," Clark wrote in his journal. "This man at all times gave us proofs of his firmness and Determined resolution to doe Service of his Countrey and honor to himself. . ."

As the crew inched upstream, the Missouri toughened the group. They fought the river, floundering in treacherous sand and mud. Frantically they pushed off snags, and crept upstream. One man "got snakebit." Men suffered sunstroke, rested, and went on. They relearned military discipline. One man received 50 lashes for drinking on duty, another a hundred for falling asleep on watch. And there was horseplay which the journals mentioned when it developed into a fistfight.

Ice stopped the expedition in the winter of 1804-5 near a village of Mandan Indians in North Dakota. The stately looking Mandan people were farmers who lived in permanent towns of earth-covered lodges. Near one of these towns, Lewis and Clark's men built two cabins with stone fireplaces. They called their camp Fort Mandan.

Here Lewis and Clark hired a new guide, a French trapper named Toussaint Charbonneau.

With Charbonneau came his wife, a girl about 16 years old destined to become one of the most famous women in American history. It is doubtful if any other American woman has had more monuments erected in her honor than the Indian lady Sacajawea. Several repose in Montana: one at Fort Benton, another at Three Forks.

Lewis and Clark particularly wanted Sacajawea to accompany them to the Rocky Mountains because of her background. Sacajawea was a Snake Indian from what is now western Montana who had been stolen as a child by an enemy tribe. She knew the mountains and the Snake language. Perhaps she could serve as an interpreter.

Before the 1805 spring weather broke up the ice on the Missouri, Sacajawea—whom Lewis and Clark nicknamed Janey—gave birth to a baby boy in an earthen Mandan lodge while snow fell outside. A French trader who had happened to be in camp told Captain Lewis that if she drank powdered rattlesnake rattle it might ease the childbirth. They had tried it and the child was born ten minutes later. Now the expedition had both a girl and an infant. Baptiste, or Pomp, went along in a basket on her mother's back.

On April 27, 1805 the expedition crossed the 104th meridian and entered what is now Montana. Here was a hostile environment, and the explorers wrote of the crusty alkali beds, the prickly cactus spines, the shifting sands, and impoverished bottomlands. Lewis classified the land as "truly a desert barren country." They wrote differently, however, about the abundance of wildlife.

"The whol face of the country" wrote Lewis, "was covered with herds of Buffaloe, Elk and Antelopes; deer are also abundant, but keep themselves more concealed in the woodland. The buffaloe, Elk and Antelope are so gentle that we pass near them while feeding, without appearing to excite any alarm among them; and when we attract their attention, they frequently approach us more nearly to discover what we are, and in some instances pursue us considerable distance apparently with that view."

As those in the expedition continued across what is now Montana, they saw abundant game: buffalo, elk, deer, antelope, beaver, porcupine, coyote, muskrat, prairie dog, and bighorn sheep. Birds filled the skies. Lewis and Clark observed hawks, owls, geese, ducks, white pelicans, blue

The Lewis and Clark Journals said that bison covered "The whole face of the country." Alan Carey.

herons, and majestic golden eagles. They made the first report of the grizzly bears of the Northwest. It took ten bullets to kill one grizzly that weighed 600 pounds and stood eight feet seven inches tall.

Early in June, in what is now central Montana, they reached a fork in the river. Which was the Missouri? It was decided that both should be checked. The party knew that there was a great waterfall somewhere in this part of the Missouri, or so they had been told by the Indians. Traveling up the south fork, Lewis and his men heard the noise of falling water and saw spray "arise above the plain like a column of smoke." Lewis ran down a hill and from a rock ledge looked out on the Great Falls of the Missouri.

It took the party two weeks to carry their boats around the long series of waterfalls and rapids.

*Above: Rattlesnakes were so frequently encountered that they were seldom mentioned in the journals. Robert Gildart.*

*Left: Grizzlies plagued Lewis and Clark along the Montana portion of the Missouri. Biologists speculate the Missouri River grizzlies may have been endowed with a more aggressive temperament than today's bear. Michael H. Francis.*

*Below: Eagle Creek, a Corps of Discovery campsite. Robert Gildart*

*Right: Headwaters of the Missouri —an aerial view of the Madison, Jefferson and Gallatin rivers. The politically astute Lewis advised President Jefferson the explorers had labored long to find a river worthy of his name. Lawrence Dodge.*

*Below right: Great Falls of the Missouri, the largest of the five falls Lewis and Clark circumvented during a three-week portage. 1907 photograph courtesy Boston and Montana Consolidated Copper and Silver Mining Co.*

16

To compound the problems of the portage, the remote area seemed haunted with strange forces and bad omens. Sacajawea got sick and almost died. Rattlesnakes were common; mosquitoes and gnats were legion. Buffalo came here to drink and to cross the river, and some were swept over the falls, their carcasses to rot. The area smelled, and grizzlies were attracted. Most all of the men were chased at one time or another, some of them more than once. Only on Independence Day did they find a reprieve from their work, whereupon they finished off the whiskey.

On July 15, the corps finally completed its portage around the Great Falls of the Missouri. It had taken from June 21 to July 15 to complete the trek and was considered by both captains to be the most strenuous work yet. Clark had written that "the men has to haul with all their strength wate and art, maney times every man all catching the grass and knobes and stones with their hands to give them more force in drawing on the Canoes and Loads, and notwithstanding the coolness of the air in high presperation and every halt, those not employed in reparing the course, are asleep in a moment, maney limping from the soreness of the feet some become fa(i)nt for a fiew moments, but no man complains all go chearfully on. To state the fatigues of this party would take up more of the journal than other notes which I find scarcely time to set down."

Here again both captains note the abundance of wildlife. Clark wrote that "the bison numbered ten thousand." And Lewis remarked about the grizzlies, which had become troublesome. Said the captain, "I do not think it prudent to send one man alone on an errand of any kind." Both captains noted that one of these "white bears" charged Joseph Fields and that he was able to escape only by leaping into the river and crouching under an overhanging bank. Another chased Drewyer for a hundred yards after he had shot it through the heart.

Several days after leaving the Great Falls, they passed through the Gates of the Mountains. On July 25, they reached the Three Forks, which they considered to be the source of the Missouri. They named the three rivers the Madison, Gallatin and Jefferson in honor of the Secretary of State, Secretary of the Treasury, and President of the United States respectively.

But now, ahead of them loomed the vast Rocky Mountains. At that time no one had any idea of the size of the Rocky Mountain chain. Lewis and Clark expected it might take them a day or two to pass over the "height of land" at the source of the Missouri. Instead, it was a month before they reached the Continental Divide. With Sacajawea's help, they obtained horses from the Snake Indians and pushed on west.

The explorers saw the Pacific Ocean in November of 1805, a year and a half after they started up the Missouri. They spent the winter of 1805-6 in log cabins near the coast of what is now Washington.

Bitterroot, the state flower, has as its scientific name Lewisia Rediviva, a living reference to Captain Lewis' botanical prowess. Will Kerling.

In the spring they again passed through Montana. Physically, their labors were considerably easier, but one dramatic episode occurred that was to have disastrous effects on fur trappers and involved several members of the expedition.

Near present day Cut Bank, Montana, along Cut Bank Creek, Lewis made what was to be his most serious error in judgement. He had split from Clark who was directed to explore the Yellowstone River, and with a small assemblage of men had entered the country of the Blackfeet and encountered a small band. With him were Reuben Fields and George Drewyer.

Lewis erred by misinterpreting the band's amicable gestures. During the night, Lewis fell into a deep sleep rather than remaining alert. He awoke to a scuffle in which Drewyer was wrestling for possession of his rifle. One of the horses was being stolen by a Blackfeet Indian, and Lewis shot him through the belly. Wrote Lewis, "he fell to his knees and on his wright elbow from which position he partly raised himself up and fired at me, and turning himself about crawled in behind a rock which was a few feet from him. He overshot me, being bareheaded I felt the wind of his bullet very distinctly."

The Indian died, and for almost half a century the Blackfeet would be hostile toward the white man.

When the expedition finally returned to the "old" United States, the local citizens were surprised. Not realizing the distances these men had to travel, Americans were sure they had perished in the wilderness. When the explorers arrived paddling in their boats toward the village of St. Louis on September 23, 1806, it was as if the party had returned from the dead. There was also great rejoicing to the east as the news of the success of the expedition reached President Jefferson.

The expedition traveled in Montana about six months of the total time and consumed about one-half of the total distance explored. The Missouri served as the highway for the first American explorers of the Louisiana Territory. It also furnished extensive knowledge of the fur resources of the upper Missouri. The journals reported on the trade already existing and estimated potential development. Construction of posts at strategic centers was recommended. The explorers considered that the first of these might well be at Council Bluffs and that another in the Dakotas might break the British trade with the Mandans. Lewis and Clark also urged a post at the confluence of the Yellowstone and the Missouri, and one on the upper Yellowstone, which was rich in "animals of the fur kind." A fort at the mouth of the Marias, which impressed them with its spring flood tide, would furnish "a safe and direct communication to that productive country of furs exclusively enjoyed at present by the subjects of his Britanic Majesty." Another post at Three Forks where the Flathead and Bannock trade could be controlled, was also considered to be advantageous.

And so began the fur era.

# The Fur Trade

*Men died on the Missouri not for metal, but in search of fur gold from beaver such as these. Photo credits left to right: Alan Carey. Tom Ulrich. Alan Carey.*

## Fur Gold

To the mountain men, the beaver was "fur gold," the most valuable commodity on earth, an animal for which they would kill.

The feature of the animal that lured men west was a soft, fine, luxurious brown pelt. The treated fur was transformed into helmets for men in the British army—and hats for the man who considered himself a real Dapper Dan.

The first step in trapping was to smear bait on the trap. Trappers called the bait their "medicine." The bait was the yellowish-brown, creamy glandular secretion of the beaver itself, musky and pungent. It was obtained from the musk glands present in both sexes.

The hunter then prepared a bed on the bottom of a stream or pond and fastened his trap down securely by means of a pole with an attached short chain which held the trap under water even when sprung. Death by drowning was the quarry's lot.

A pack of 100 pounds of beaver pelts sold in 1804 for $180.00. A prime pelt at the opening of the American trade commanded $6.00. The price was $5.00 in the 1820s, down to $4.00 by the 1830s and plummeted to $2.00 in the 1840s. One beaver pack served as the basic exchange unit of the American fur trade.

Beaver also were considered a delicacy among hunters. Henry R. Schoolcraft penned what Stanley Vestal in his book *The Missouri* considered the classic description of the best dainty known to the Missouri hunter:

"We were invited at supper, as a particular mark of respect, to partake of a roasted beaver's tail . . . Having heard much said among hunters concerning the peculiar flavour and delicious richness of this dish, I was highly gratified in having an opportunity of judging for myself, and accepted with avidity the offer of our host. The tail of this animal, unlike every other part of it, and of every other animal of the numerous tribe of quadrupeds, is covered with a thick scaly skin, resembling in texture certain fish, and in shape analogous to a paper-folder, or the bow of a lady's corset, tapering a little toward the end, and pyramidal on the lateral edges. It is cooked by roasting before the fire, when the skin peels off, and it is eaten simply with salt. It has a mellow, luscious taste, melting in the mouth somewhat like marrow, and being in taste something intermediate between that and a boiled perch. To this compound flavour of fish and marrow it has, in the way in which hunters eat it, a slight disagreeable smell of oil. Could this be removed by some culinary process, it would undoubtedly be received on the table of the epicure with great eclat."

Like all furs, beaver hair was of varying form and quality. Whatever the grade, all beaver hats were made from the soft underfur shaved from the hide, sorted to size and glued onto the headpiece. However, as with other articles of clothing, styles were destined eventually to change and, with the appearance of the silk hat toward the end of the 1820s, the beaver market dropped alarmingly. But, because of the beaver, and the mountain man who risked his life for this golden fur, the upper Missouri became a bawdy, romantic chapter in American history.

19

*For almost 30 years Blackfeet prevented fur trappers from penetrating the richest stretches of the upper Missouri. Shown here is the Jefferson River about a mile from the Missouri's headwaters. Robert Gildart.*

## Fur Companies and their Forts

During the first two centuries of exploration and exploitation of the fur resources of America, no trade had been established in what is now Montana. The semi-arid Dakotas served as a barrier to traders and trappers seeking new fields. The bison of the Great Plains had skins that the French thought for a time could be used for the manufacture of wool and leather. But the wool was too expensive to produce, and the skins were not suitable for the French market.

Not until after 1800 did the fur trade extend to the Missouri headwaters. Rival Canadian companies pushed vigorously upriver and into the wilderness. The oldest and richest of these was the Hudson Bay Company, chartered by the English crown in 1670. Its grant included the whole basin of Hudson Bay, whose southwest borders overlapped into the Missouri River country. Rival companies were ousted by the Hudson Bay Company and, for awhile, this gigantic enterprise held sway over the entire area.

In the United States, one rival of the Canadian companies, John Jacob Astor, was developing plans to exploit the fur trade of the far Northwest. Astor was a German immigrant who used the fur trade to build the greatest fortune in 19th century America and to establish the first American monopoly.

Astor became interested in the furs at the headwaters of the Missouri. To exploit this interest, he sought, with limited success, the cooperation of the prominent fur traders in St. Louis. That town, then an outpost at the mouth of the Missouri, was the undisputed center of the fur industry from 1807 to 1843. From there, most wilderness expeditions set forth, and from there trade goods entered the world market. Astor endeavored to retain for American use the local leaders of the international fur competition between Spain, France and the United States. Among the most prominent of these traders were Auguste and Pierre Choteau, Pierre Menard, Andrew Henry and Manuel Lisa. These men sent their trappers up the Missouri into the Dakotas where they secured a rich harvest.

In Montana, exploration and harvesting began in earnest in 1806 when John Colter, an outstanding private soldier, requested and received an honorable discharge from the returning Lewis and Clark Expedition. He received his discharge at the Mandan villages in present-day North Dakota, where the explorers had spent the first winter of their campaign. The day before, Colter had met two dedicated hunters bound for the tributaries of the upper Missouri. Colter joined the two men and spent the winter in the Yellowstone River Valley. When the spring of 1807 arrived, Colter abandoned the idea of another trek up the Missouri and began a return trip down the river.

That same year, Manuel Lisa, an energetic though controversial entrepreneur destined to make a name for himself in the annals of the early west, formed the Missouri Fur Company and organized the first fur expedition into the upper Missouri. George Drouillard, from the Lewis and Clark Expedition, was Lisa's chief of operations. Near the mouth of the Platte River in present-day Nebraska, Lisa met John Colter, and, for a second time, the adventurer was induced to forgo the prospect of comforts associated with civilization and return to the wilderness. The group continued up the Missouri and the Yellowstone rivers to the mouth of the Bighorn. Here, in the heartland of the Crow Nation, the first American trading post and the first building in present-day Montana were constructed on the Yellowstone. Lisa, the group's ever-modest leader, named the fort in honor of himself; it became known as Lisa's Fort or Fort Manuel.

Lisa returned to St. Louis the following year. So successful was his venture that he was able to wrangle the necessary capital for a second, considerably larger trip, up the Missouri. In 1809, 150 men departed from St. Louis with the intention of expanding trading and trapping in the most dangerous of all areas—the hostile Blackfeet country near the upper three forks of the Missouri. Here, under the direction of John Colter, the group, which now included two of Lisa's business partners, quickly erected a fort. This was prime beaver country and still is, as those who float this portion of the Missouri soon discover. At the time its waters included what was perhaps the best habitat to be found along the Missouri. The party appeared on the verge of great prosperity. But their luck was of short duration.

Colter and his old expedition companion, Potts, were caught one morning near the three forks by the Blackfeet. Potts was killed instantly. But Colter had shown extreme bravery, and the Blackfeet thought they would amuse themselves.

As the legend goes, the Indians asked Colter if he was fleet of foot. Colter responded that he was slow, "like a crippled bird." So persuasive was Colter that they decided to permit him to run for his life. Stripping Colter naked, they gave him a headstart.

Colter ran like a madman, ignoring the prickle pear and rocks that must have dug into his feet—exerting himself so hard that according to him blood began to gush from his nose and to cover his face. His efforts enabled him to outdistance all but one exceedingly swift warrior who began to gain on the agile Colter. When the warrior was almost within striking distance, Colter stopped and wheeled. The surprised warrior stumbled, and dropped his spear. Colter snatched it from the ground and drove it into the warrior, pinning him to the ground. Colter then continued running until, at last, he came to the banks of the Missouri. Colter hid in some driftwood while hundreds of Blackfeet searched the banks, even stepping on the huge raft of entangled wood. But Colter was well hidden; he had broken off a hollow reed through which he might breathe.

When night fell, Colter pulled himself from the murky Missouri River waters and began to walk, hiding now and then—shivering. He was alone and naked.

For eight days Colter wandered through the wilderness. But at long last he stumbled into Manuel Lisa's new fort on the Bighorn, finding food, relief, and a place in the roll call of American heroes. Today, passes, canyons and waters which eventually drain into the Missouri, have been named after this adventurer.

The year after Colter's run, Drouillard heard the story when he arrived at the fort. He too was trapping for Lisa, who had sent him back to the three forks area. On the morning of April 2, 1810, the powerful Blackfeet surprised and killed an isolated group of trappers. One month later, George Drouillard was spotted in the same area and, though he fought like a madman, was killed and scalped.

Two years later, the War of 1812 took men and resources away from the fur trade and for a few years all was quiet on the western front. Manual Lisa died, but by 1814 the Missouri Fur Company was again delivering pelts to St. Louis. But these were taken from tributaries of the Yellowstone, not from the Blackfeet-dominated three forks area.

Five years later, in 1819, trappers again were pushing into the upper Missouri country, and again they confronted Indians. In May of 1823, about 400 Blackfeet attacked a group of 29 trappers who had taken furs from the Madison, Jefferson and Gallatin rivers. Once again the combative Blackfeet curtailed the fur trade in that region of the Missouri River.

In October of 1828, a new man entered the scene. His name was Kenneth McKenzie, described by fur historian Hiram M. Chittenden as "the ablest leader that the American Fur Company ever possessed." History records him as saying "I cannot bear to hear or read the word impossible applied to business affairs." He applied these same sentiments to his work along the Missouri, beginning by leading James Kipp and a construction crew to the confluence of the Missouri and Yellowstone rivers. There he founded a fur trade post that would become known as Fort Union.

As soon as his headquarters was established, McKenzie turned his attention to expanding farther up the Missouri into Montana—the land of the Blackfeet.

*Not far from where old Fort Union was located, this is near today's Bainville. Jim Romo.*

McKenzie desperately wanted the upper Missouri trade. But the Blackfeet had been trading with the British. Luckily, a former employee of the Hudson Bay Company was now in the trade of the Upper Missouri Outfit, and the man spoke Blackfeet. McKenzie requested the man to contact the tribe. He sent him upstream with many presents and a promise to build a trading house for the Blackfeet in their own country.

True to his word, McKenzie sent James Kipp and 25 men to the junction of the Marias and Missouri rivers. A small fort was erected and named Fort Piegan. It was the white man's first foothold in the area where the elaborate town of Fort Benton would be established years later.

That winter Kipp and his men engaged in a thriving exchange of trading with the previously hostile Blackfeet. In the spring, he and his men left the fort with their goods and journeyed downstream to Fort Union. Shortly after his departure, Indians burned the fort for unknown reasons. But the fort had lasted a year, and it was a start at trading in a hostile area.

In 1832, a man by the name of D.D. Mitchell was sent back to the area with instructions to construct another fort. Not liking the location Kipp had selected, Mitchell chose a spot on the south bank—opposite the Marias River. The construction period of the new post was a suspenseful one for the trappers. Thousands of suspicious Blackfeet were on hand, and the men worked frantically to erect the fort before there was an outbreak of hostilities. During the night they slept aboard their keelboat; guards were on duty around the clock. Extreme boldness and tact were required on the part of Mitchell to pacify the Blackfeet during the construction period, but eventually the fort was complete. Once inside what they dubbed Fort McKenzie, trappers felt safe.

## King of the Missouri

While the later forts of McKenzie, Chardon, and Lewis vacillated between the active and inactive, earlier Fort Union had stood out as the hub of the fur trade of its time. It was considered the finest post on the Missouri, and quite possibly, the most lavish in the entire West.

Located on the north bank, it was about 25 feet from the river and six miles from the mouth of the Yellowstone. Around it was a sprawling prairie that gave way on the west and north to rolling hills and bluffs. It was built for protection rather than military use, and it functioned well for trade.

It was conceived by McKenzie who had impeccable tastes. McKenzie lived in a style worthy of the title he acquired soon after his arrival—"King of the Upper Missouri," or simply, "King McKenzie."

McKenzie played the part. He dressed for dinner at a table set with china and silverware. His subordinates sat at the long table in descending order of importance. Meat, vegetables, dairy products, and good bread were served at his table, with coffee, tea, and wine. The ordinary laborers, sitting at a separate table, also ate plentifully, but of a restricted fare.

McKenzie hosted many influential guests in these palatial surroundings, including John James Audubon, famous naturalist-painter. Later Audubon wrote in his journals about his arrival: "We came in sight of the fort at five o'clock, and reached it at seven . . . We were saluted (by cannon) from Fort Union, and we fired guns in return . . . The moment we had arrived, the gentlemen of the fort came down on horseback, and appeared quite a cavalcade . . . We walked to the fort and drank some first-rate port wine."

In an attempt to circumvent the strict liquor importation laws, McKenzie ordered a whiskey still from St. Louis. It was installed at the fort in 1833, an unfortunate move. The needed corn was supplied by the company's own gardens in present-day Iowa and from Indian harvests brought up from the Mandan villages. Proudly, the King reported to St. Louis that his liquor was of a very fine quality. As proof, he drank it himself and offered it to his guests. But that fall, following an evening meal with the King in late summer, a competitor informed authorities of the illegal activity. The distillery was dismantled the following year. Even though American Fur officials were perfectly aware of the existence and history of the still, McKenzie was made the scapegoat. The action saved the company's license and McKenzie was retired. As author A.B. Guthrie might say, "McKenzie had gotten too big for God." It is estimated that he accumulated a fortune of $150,000 during his fur-trade career.

He returned to Fort Union for several brief visits and a short term as a substitute manager.

By 1834, the fur trade was starting to decline. Silk hats were gaining popularity in Europe, diminishing the demand for beaver-felt hats. The smallpox epidemic among Indians had exacted so severe a toll that the trapping-trading native was hardly available. The Mandans were obliterated and the Assinaboines died by the hundreds; thousands of Blackfeet perished and their strength was forever broken. From the 1850s to the 1900s lack of market demand, increasing settlement, homestead activity, the Indian wars, and the discovery of gold further crippled the fur industry and Fort Union fell into disuse. Today, the site of the fort serves as a staging area for a National Park Living History Program.

## Crime and Attrition

Fort McKenzie lasted about ten years and during that time was the location of numerous disreputable acts. One atrocious crime eventually proved to be its downfall.

In the winter of 1842-43 a plan was initiated calling for all members of the trading post to fall upon the unsuspecting Indians. They were to kill all they could and confiscate their property. But the plan was only partially effective and succeeded more in instilling in the Indians a desire for vengeance than it did in acquiring material possessions. They succeeded to the extent that all trappers were driven out of Fort McKenzie. In the wake of the hostilities, Fort McKenzie was burned, eventually lost its old name, and became known by the French word Brule, or "burned" fort.

Today the name persists as Brule Bottom—a name reminiscent of violence. But nothing is left to remind the floater of today that this was once a site of great treachery and deceit. In fact, the converse is true. Here is an area of incredible silence and tranquility. Only natural sounds, such as the croak of a great blue heron lifting ponderously into the air, break the silence.

In 1843, men from Fort McKenzie began erecting another fort. Prudently, they moved far downstream to the Judith River where they built Fort Chardon. Chardon was the man who had initiated the uncalled for attack against the Indians.

Because of the hostile situation along the upper Missouri River, the American Fur Company rehired one of its more dependable and proven men. The man, Alexander Culbertson, returned upstream and began the process of reestablishing good working relations with Indians. He started his attempt by abandoning and burning Fort Chardon and establishing a new post 12 miles above the current site of Fort Benton. The fort was built on the north bank of the Missouri and was named Fort Lewis in honor of Captain Meriwether Lewis.

With Chardon now out of the way, Culbertson soon was able to reestablish trade with the Blackfeet. The site of Fort Lewis, however, proved unacceptable. In the spring of 1846, the post was dismantled and moved downriver to the site where the town of Fort Benton currently reposes. In 1848, company books began listing the site as Fort Benton, but it wasn't officially christened by that name until December 25, 1850. The dedication was to honor Senator Hart Benton of Missouri—a man who for many years had aided various fur companies headquartered at St. Louis.

At each of these posts, a method of trade had been instituted to protect the traders. Through a narrow wooden grate, too small for an irate Indian to reach the trader, the goods appeared in exchange for furs. Necessity dictated these defensive measures since much of the fur trade depended on outlawed whiskey, the most effective means of luring Indians to the trading post.

*Top: Missouri Indian trade items as displayed at Fort Union. Robert Gildart.*

*Bottom left: The currency of the upper Missouri, beaver pelt in Fort Benton Museum. Robert Gildart.*

*Middle: The mothership of the fur trader was the keelboat. This is a replica of "Mandan," used in the movie The Big Sky, and now located at Fort Benton. Tim Church.*

*Right: Site of old Fort Benton. Tim Church.*

*All Karl Bodmer artwork, this page and at right courtesy: The InterNorth Art Foundation, Joslyn Art Museum, Omaha, Nebraska*

One year after Fort McKenzie was constructed a keelboat arrived at the fort. On board were the first two men ever to visually record the upper Missouri River. One man was in his mid-fifties; the other in his early twenties.

The older of the two was a prince who had served as a major general during the Napoleonic Wars. He was also a scholar. He had hired his Swiss companion because of the younger man's exceptional ability to portray exquisite detail.

Prince Alexander Phillip Maximilian of Wied-Neuwied and artist Karl Bodmer arrived at the new fort on August 9, 1833, to see the American flag waving near the mouth of a river Lewis had named Marias in honor of his cousin Maria. They would spend five weeks at the fort and, during that time, Bodmer would paint such eloquent scenes that they would later be reproduced in a fine-art book.

One of Bodmer's paintings is said to have been of Wolf Calf, who later claimed to have been a member of the small Piegan party whose dawn attempt to steal Lewis's horses on the upper Marias precipitated the only Indian fight of that entire expedition.

Bodmer and Maximilian also were eyewitnesses to a Blackfeet battle. At daybreak on August 28th, they were awakened by the sound of gunfire. Running to the elevated platform just inside the fort's palisade, they saw the prairie covered with Indians. A full-scale battle was in progress between a small band of Piegan traders camped outside the fort and 600 or more Assiniboine and Cree Indians. The fort's leaders decided to assist the Piegan traders, and it is reported that the old ex-general took a shot or two at the attackers.

During the melee, Bodmer was active with his paints. His rendition depicts with vividness the ferocity of the struggle.

*Top : Along the White Cliffs.*
*Bottom: Bodmer created one of the best, first-hand visual accounts of Indian warfare after witnessing an attack by Assiniboine and Cree on Blackfeet camped at Fort McKenzie on August 28, 1833.*

# The Legend of Mike Fink

When men were recruited for a fur trapping and trading expedition to Fort Musselshell on the Missouri, a number of American boatmen volunteered. Among them was the celebrated Mike Fink, who by his great strength, pugilistic powers, queer pranks and skill with the rifle, had already obtained the widest notoriety of any in his class. As he himself so often said, "I'm little, but the almightiest man on the river anyhow. I'm a Salt River Roarer! I'm chuck full of fight and I love the women!"

Fink certainly was a ladies' man for while most of his fellows may have boasted of having a woman in every port, Fink customarily kept one aboard and his methods of insuring fidelity were unique. Once when a Fink damsel winked at another man, the "Salt River Roarer" set her clothes afire; she saved herself by jumping into the river.

In Montana, Mike's good fortune, however, was as ephemeral as a ripple on the surface of the Missouri. Before long, his quarrelsome disposition brought him into conflict with a Mr. Henry, one of Manuel Lisa's former business partners, and the man who, in 18, who was in charge of continuing the expedition to the mouth of the Musselshell River.

Fink's difficulties originated in his exorbitant demands for whiskey. Refused permission to continue imbibing, an enraged Mike raised his rifle and fired into a cask. Then, with his companions, the mightiest man on the Missouri freely helped himself to the escaping contents.

Matters went from bad to worse. Under the constant influence of whiskey, Mike grew increasingly despondent. At last he declared he would no longer live at the fort, and, accompanied only by a youth named Carpenter, dug a hole in the river bank of the Missouri in which they passed the winter.

Come spring they were visited by friends from the fort who brought along a supply of liquor. They wanted to rouse Mike out of his hole. Soon there commenced a grand spree. Carpenter and Mike served as the principal participants. Brains addled; the results soon proved disastrous.

Carpenter was an orphan whom Mike had adopted and, as Mike expressed it, "I loved like my own cub." He had instructed the youth in all his own accomplishments and, under his training, Carpenter had become as expert with therifle as Mike himself—and Mike's marksmanship was something to behold.

To exhibit their skill and confidence in one another, it was their custom to take turns shooting a cup of whiskey from the other's head.

The winter had been long and, as the story goes, acrimonious. The two had spent the long months vying for the attention of an Indian woman, and now it appeared as though they were anxious to show their good will toward one another by resuming their customary mode of target practice. Filling a cup with whiskey, Fink walked off some 40 yards. With a boisterous laugh and whiskey-glazed eye, Carpenter complied, took his position, and fired. The can fell and the spectators cheered. But Fink only clutched his rifle and gazed strangely at Carpenter. The ball had grazed his head, and the conviction flashed through Mike that Carpenter had meant to kill him.

Undaunted, Fink took his turn. Lifting the rifle slowly, and sighting through what must have been eyes blurred by whiskey, Fink took careful aim.

The rest is in the history books and well documented. Fink blew out the brains of his "cub."

Fink mourned. "Carpenter," he said, "you have spilled the whiskey." This eulogy proved too much for one of Carpenter's friends who hauled out his pistol and shot Fink through the heart.

Today their bodies lie side by side along the Missouri River between Ft. Union and Ft. Buford, their ghosts still swaggering as each full moon rises over the river's rippling waters.

*This statue at the entrance to Fort Buford symbolizes the plight of the Indian confronting the end of life on the open hunting grounds and, worse, the diseases such as small pox brought up river by advancing traders. Robert Gildart.*

*Today the Missouri's shores host the annual Brockton Powwow near Poplar. Robert Gildart.*

## Smallpox

The fur trade introduced into the upper Missouri the deadliest pacifier of the Indian and particularly the Blackfoot. It was not articles for trade, the military, or improved weaponry but smallpox. In 1837, this disease visited Fort McKenzie and the resulting scenes were as pathetic as those from a Nazi concentration camp. The dreaded disease assumes an extra dimension of horror when one considers that historians have some evidence that the smallpox epidemic which struck the upper Missouri River was intentional. Infected blankets were offered in trade to Indians along the Missouri River who had no natural immunity. That summer the effects of the disease were felt at various villages along the Missouri, but mainly at Fort McKenzie, where a large part of the Blackfeet nation was gathered.

When the steamer carrying the blankets arrived, many aboard already were infected. Alexander Culbertson, a compassionate man destined to make a broad mark on the slate of Montana history, went to a camp of about 500 lodges and attempted to explain why the Indians should stay away from the keelboat with its trade goods. But the Indians had never experienced the effects of smallpox and suspected that Culbertson was attempting to swindle them out of their rightful opportunity to trade. Culbertson then asked the chiefs to be aware that he had warned them and that they should not hold the fort accountable for what might happen.

Nearly everyone at the fort, including Culbertson, caught the disease. Though Culbertson survived, the Blackfeet were devastated. The disease spread throughout their entire nation and no one realized the extent until Culbertson went to find out why no Blackfeet were coming to Fort McKenzie for trade. It wasn't until he reached Three Forks that he fully understood. Here, he found a village. Though lodges were present, no sound came from them as he approached. All he found were two demented women crawling among the corpses.

The manner in which the Blackfeet died has best been described by historian Bernard DeVoto in his book, *Across the Wide Missouri*: "So there came a point when the savage mind understood that it had misconceived the universe: its theory or reality would not hold. When the bases of thought are proved in error, nothing is left but frenzy . . . Two sick braves debate the manliest way; one cuts his own throat, the other forces an arrow down his throat into his lungs. A brave shoots his wife, then disembowels himself. A newly widowed squaw kills her two children and hangs herself. A young man has his mother dig a grave, walks out to it with his father's help, and lies down in it. When the son of another one dies, he tells his wife that they ought to join the boy in the after-land; when she agrees he shoots her, reloads his gun, takes the muzzle in his mouth, and pulls the trigger with his toe."

And so passed many of the Blackfeet in the year of 1837. Thereafter, the countryside around Fort McKenzie finally would be open, though not safe, for the fur trade.

# Living History

When the sun is at an oblique angle and an early morning fog is rising from the Missouri River, motorists driving along a dusty road near the Montana-North Dakota border are greeted by a scene that compels them to pause for a second look. Ahead through the mist, loom tepees, as ephemeral in appearance as is the smoke that belches from their vents. Peering closer through the mist, one sees a hubbub of activity. The setting beckons.

"Welcome," says a gaunt man wearing a black vest, felt hat and white trousers tucked into a pair of knee-high boots. "This is where old Fort Union was located, site of the largest and most significant fur post along the Missouri. We ask that you stay and explore our living quarters and engage in a few of the activities. Try, for example, making a fire with flint and steel, or throwing an axe at a large stump and making it stick. If you stay long enough there will be a black powder shooting match."

The man's name is Tim Duffy, a master's degree candidate in history who is in charge of the Living History program conducted at this location by the National Park Service. The man is well informed, and I left feeling a kinship with the independent men I had grown to idolize after reading A.B. Guthrie's *Big Sky*. Mountain man Boone Caudill, although a creation of Guthrie's vivid imagination, surely must have walked through this most strategic of all fur forts. In the book he met McKenzie and other significant men who made these trading posts a highly profitable business. Caudill's mentor, Dick Summers had not liked the "Bogeway" McKenzie. He had become too big and "God don't cotton to the competition."

Still, McKenzie, and other mountain men, had helped initiate the rise of an independent United States and the growth and development of the Louisiana Purchase.

Today, much of this period is relived at this National Park Service historical area. Plans call for the reconstruction of a replica of old Fort Union. In the meantime, tepees surrounding remnants of the structure are present. Inside and wandering around the grounds are mountain men clad in leather buckskins. Visitors joining these programs discover what life may have been like during the age of adventure. They also have the opportunity to learn how to defend themselves with an axe, though that is no simple lesson. There is much more to the art than just grasping the weapon by the handle and hurling it into space, though the mountain men make it appear that easy. It requires dexterity, coordination and judgement. Distance and the number of revolutions the axe will revolve prior to striking the object are necessary considerations. But the free traders are willing to help you for as long as your arm endures. And, if you wait long enough, you might experience a black powder firing contest or be around to welcome other mountain men who descend on Fort Union for annual get-togethers.

*The Living History Program operated by the National Park Service at the site of old Ft. Union just over the Montana border in North Dakota recreates the fur era of the 1830s. Robert Gildart.*

# The Military Forts

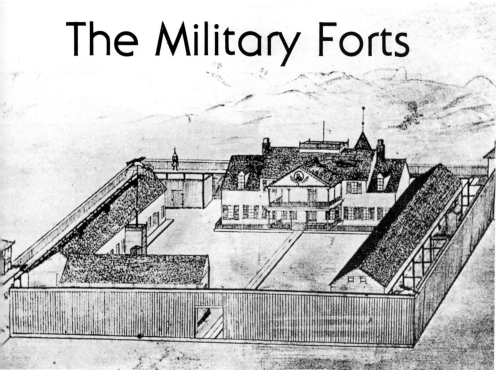

Fort Union, 1864.

Fort Buford today. Robert Gildart.

## Fort Buford

Old Fort Union was a fur fort and, when it had accomplished its function, was dismantled, carried upstream a distance of several miles, reassembled, and became a military fort. In this new location it was named Fort Buford. Today, the fort can be found about a mile east of the Montana-North Dakota border, at the confluence of the Missouri and Yellowstone rivers.

Like other military forts of the time, its mission was to protect settlers from the depredation of Indians as their families attempted to forge a living in a hostile environment.

According to E.J. Duffey, father of the young master's degree candidate employed seasonally at Ft. Union, Ft. Buford provided this function, sometimes well, at other times not so well.

As a curator of the Ft. Buford Historical Area for more a decade, Duffey knows history well and

has an avid enthusiasm for "his fort." With his goatee styled beard, weather-lined face and dreamy eyes he looks a bit like the pictures of Abe Lincoln.

I met "E.J." on a rainy June day, and we began a several-hour-long discussion.

"Soldiers had it rough around here," said Duffey. "And so did the civilians living nearby. It was a tough place, men deserting, men overdrinking. Take a look at our graveyard and you will see what I mean." Men at Buford had died of everything imaginable. Suicide, murder, consumption, road agents and inebriation were a few of the most common forms of death.

Duffey knew intimately the story concerning the demise of one man and his companion. It had been anything but glorious.

According to an old Fort Buford log, which Duf-

fey dug out, a man by the name of Roche and a black man known only as Tom were assigned by the North West Fur Company to bring the last hay loads from the Little Muddy. They had left their guns at Fort Buford because things were quiet. The next day the search party found a hay load. The horse teams were gone, but not the mangled bodies of the two hay loaders. Laying grotesquely were the corpses; they had been beaten to death with whiffle trees taken from one of their own wagons. Twenty-one arrows were sticking in each body. Both had been scalped and their bodies horribly mutilated.

Fort Buford, according to Duffey, was the site where a number of famous Indian chiefs were interned for brief periods of time. Buildings that still stand confined Rain-In-The-Face, Chief Crow King, Sitting Bull, Chief Gall and Chief Joseph.

The old Missouri was a turbulent land!

## Camp Cooke

On a hot blistering day in July, a well known Montana historian directed our canoes down a small web-like series of channels formed by the Missouri River. We were well off the main course a short distance above the Judith Landing looking for "an indentation in the bank." Several times we had to wade, pulling our crafts over gravel bars too shallow for even our lightly loaded canoes. Our director knew the area well and, though the way seemed obscure, he soon pointed with his paddle to a small opening in the brush.

The group leader was Dr. Harrison Lane, retired professor emeritus from Northern Montana College located at Havre. Lane had not settled into the easy chair in retirement. Not surprisingly, much of his work is beginning to center around the Missouri River.

Since his retirement Dr. Lane has published a book concerning the flight of Nez Perce. Much of it centers around the Missouri. But of greater pertinence for floaters is his continued interest in conducting his "Floating Classroom." On these trips, each morning starts with an assemblage of canoes drifting placidly down the Missouri. Over the gurgle of the river and the scraping of canoes against one another and people straining their heads to hear what this extremely knowledgeable man has to say about the area.

During 1866-68 the power of the Indians on the Northern Plains was at its height. Chief Red Cloud and his warriors held Fort Phillip Kearny in a ring of steel and finally forced the government to abandon it and to give up the Bozeman Trail. At the same time, Fort Buford on the Upper Missouri was in a state of continuous siege. Steamboats passing up and down the river were being fired upon by lurking Indians. Numerous attacks were made upon isolated parties of woodhawkers, who supplied the boats with fuel, and upon haying parties, as well as upon horse and cattle herds. All activities had to be conducted under the protection of the various military posts established along the Missouri River. Soldiers, unless in parties, dared not go more than a short distance from their garrisons. It appeared doubtful that the government could hold the region or, if so, whether it was worth the sacrifice.

Camp Cooke was to play a vital role. Chosen in Washington D.C., it was Montana's first military fort and was built in 1866 on the mouth of the Judith River, to protect steamboat traffic from Indian attacks. Compared to some of the earlier trading "forts," the post presented a rather formidable appearance. There were two large warehouses and four large barracks, all built of cottonwood logs.

The fort lasted only until 1870 at which time the camp was abandoned and the few remaining troops moved up to Fort Benton, now a military fort, or onto Fort Shaw on the Sun River. Salvage from the buildings was used to build a trading post known as Fort Claggett; later to become Judith Landing and site of the PN ranch and ferry.

An hour or so after entering the spur channel, we pushed our way to the indentation for which we had been searching. Then, for about 30 minutes, we pushed aside brush until we came to a clearing near the Judith River. It was, as Dr. Lane said, an ideal area for a fort and a much needed fort at that.

*Above: Hunkpapa Sioux interred at Ft. Buford included (clockwise) Sitting Bull and Chiefs Gall, RainIn-The-Face, and Crow King. Courtesy Western History Museum, Denver Library.*

*Left: "Killed by Indians" was a common epitaph for soldiers stationed near the confluence of the Yellowstone and Missouri. This headstone is at Fort Buford. Robert Gildart.*

# The Diary Of
# Sarah Elizabeth Canfield

In the spring of 1867, Sarah Elizabeth Canfield ventured into untamed country, traveling by steamboat into the heart of the Indian country to join her husband Andrew Nahum Canfield. Nahum, as she called him, was a veteran of the Civil War.

The couple had been married on April 30, 1866, at Governor's Island in New York. Several months after arriving at Fort Berthold in North Dakota, they were transferred to Camp Cooke, Montana Territory.

Mrs. Canfield was at the post when it was attacked by a large party of Indians. The incident occurred in the spring of 1867 and, as with other events following her marriage, she maintained an accurate and vivid diary that recaptures these eyewitness accounts. She was 27 years old at the time, and her diary provides intimate glimpses of life in a frontier post which are seldom found in historical articles or journals.

*April 30, 1866 I now open a new chapter in my diary and begin a new life. Was married today. My husband is an officer in the Regular Army. His Reg't is stationed at New York on Governors Island. (Shortly after the marriage the duties of the army took Lt. Canfield west after which time the couple was separated for almost one full year.)*

*May 30 The Regt did not Stay long at Ft. L but are now going up the Mo. river, he does not know their destination, only they are to keep navigation open on the river. The Indians are very troublesome now.*

*Nov 13 Letters come at long intervals usually three or four at a time, as the mail is sent from Ft Berthold usually by Indian runners to Virginia City or Helena Mon Ter*

*Remains of the fireplace of the officer's quarters of old Camp Cooke. Tim Church.*

*then comes to Omaha by stage. Since navigation on the river is closed. Letters are a month or more on the way.*

*Christmas—This has been a long day for me though I was cheered by getting three letters from my husband. The last one was written Nov 5, a long time ago. But he is well and looking eagerly forward to my coming on the first boat.*

*Mar. 27—April 15, 1867 The "Deer Lodge" came up today and I am on board and starting my long journey—I occupy a stateroom with Lieut. Hogan's wife. She is going to Ft. Shaw Mon Ter where her husband is stationed with a different Batallion of the Same Regt (the 13th U.S. Infantry) to which Mr. C belongs.*

*There is also a sick lady on board. She is a full blooded Indian of the Blackfeet tribe a chiefs daughter who married a white man, a fur trader, he is immensely wealthy—They have educated their children in the states and are now returning from a visit to them and from a tour among the large cities of the country.*

*April 25. The wild flowers are beginning to bloom, and today when the boat stopped to cut wood we went ashore and gathered a few but the gentlemen armed themselves and acted as our escort, even then we did not go very far from the boat, for wild Indians are all around us. We do not often see them, but we know they are near for this morning about daylight as our boat was just starting from where it had been tied to the bank all night, (we run all night when the moon shines and the water is good) the pilot was shot at in the pilot house. As he was shot with arrows no one knew it until he was found. The Captain says he will leave the body at Ft. Rice to-morrow for burial.*

*The Clerk of the boat has just brought me three letters from Mr. C directed to my Iowa address. He said he found them in a Gunny Sack of mail which one of the men found on the bank of the river while we were gathering wood. At first I was very much frightened... The date of the last letter was early Jan. nearly four months ago...I had a hard cry over my letters, but Capt Ohlman told me not to worry, but if anything had happened to my husband, he would bring me back home all right which is very kind of him.*

*May 19. This is Sunday and a very beautiful day—I am out on deck pretending to read but my mind is not on my reading very much for the Captain has just told me that he hopes to reach Ft. Berthold tonight. Is my dear Husband alive? Am I indeed to see him soon? I am very anxious but am determined to appear calm as possible.*

*About 150 miles of the Missouri is designated as a  National Wild and Scenic River. Len Eckel.*

*May 20. When the sun rose was near enough to hear the bugle sound reville and see the dear old flag go up to the top of the flagstaff, but I did not know that Someone was on the Watchtower trying to see me at long range . . . And I was delighted to recognize him as the first man to step on the gangplank when we Stopped . . . I am at home with my dear husband . . .*

*June 26. Mr. C is ordered to Camp Cooke Montana Ter. So we are packing our trunks to be ready to go on the first boat going up Stream.*

*June 27. We are on board the "Luella" a small stern wheel boat. We are likely to be some time on the way as the river is very low and the current is very swift. There are several passengers on board and two men have their families with them going to the gold mines near Virginia City Mon Ter.*

*July 9. We passed Forts Buford and Union today . . . We are now entering Montana Ter. The river is growing smaller. One large Stream, the Yellowstone, flows into the Mo river between and opposite Buford Dakota Ter and Union Montana Ter. I do not know why the water was So turbid and yellow but we could easily follow the current as it poured into the Missouri which here is clear water with a rocky and sand bottom.*

*July 12. Saw another large herd of Buffalo swim the river today led by a large Shaggy old bull. They look so heavy and lubberly the wonder is they can swim at all.*

*July 13. We passed Ft Peck today. It is only a Fur trading post but is Strongly fortified. When the Indians (The Crows) come in to trade the gates are closed and all business is conducted through a Small opening in the wall which can be closed at a moments notice.*

*July 18. Camp Cooke, Montana, Ter. We arrived at 3:30 this P.M. As our quarters were not ready we are guests of the Commanding Officer Col Andrews . . . This Ft. is situated on the South side of the Mo. river, on the point where the Judith flows into the Mo. We have the Mo. north and the Judith east. West and South we are surrounded by the foothills of the mountains with ranges of Mountains in the distance while across the river north we have a fine view of the Bear Paw mountains a distance of about thirty miles—they seem to be*

*isolated peaks on a comparatively level Stretch of country—There are four ladies here . . . They have all been in to welcome me to the Ft and as they will remain here this winter and there are no other ladies within 60 miles of us we are likely to See a good deal of each other . . .*

*July 30. We went fishing today in the Judith river which is a beautiful clear mountain stream. Nahum caught some grasshoppers for bait and baited my hook which I threw into a quiet pool near the bank before he had time to bait his own hook. I landed on the bank a fish weighing about 5 lbs. I repeated the performance four times until we had caught three or four, we went to the Ft with fish enough to Share with the Officers.*

*Rec'd a lot of mail from the States today. How eagerly we read our home letters. The papers Some of them a month old were very new to us.*

*Sept 5. Some of the officers went hunting today. They gave us qr. of venison. Yesterday we had great excitement at the Ft. The Indians came down to within a quarter of a mile and drove off all our beef and some horses killing one man.*

*Oct. 1. The weather is getting cold. We, the ladies do not go outside the stockade but take exercise walking up and down the long porch in front of our rooms. The peak of the Mountains are now covered with snow, and we have such lovely northern lights—they can be seen almost every night, often forming a luminous arch in the heavens which lasts many hours.*

*The river is very low. No more boats will come up this fall. We are 200 miles from Helena Mon. our nearest town. One of the late boats brought from the Gallatin valley some fresh vegetables for which they charge $6.00 per bu for potatoes 30 cts a lb., for cabbage, other vegetables in proportion. We live mostly on canned goods of which the Gov't supplies an abundance. Then too we have plenty of fresh beef. On Nahum's last trip to the coal mines he bought a young cow. Now we have plenty of milk and butter. A soldier, a young Irish boy, takes care of her. He wants to learn to make butter and it might come handy if they should have to move where I could not go with them. Last night the drum beat an*

*alarm. Our sawmill was destroyed by fire. We suspect the Indians. They come around the Ft and as they seem friendly a few are allowed to come inside. I think the Col., wants to impress them with the fact that we have men enough to make it uncomfortable for any force they might bring—One day as I sat working a pair of slippers with bright wool yarn what seemed to be a cloud passed. I looked up to find two squaws with their faces against the window pane. I held it up for them to see. They laughed and chatted to each other.*

*Nov 10. We are now having cold weather. I suppose we are shut in for the winter. There is quite a supply of books and we get papers and Magazines when the mail comes. The time of night will be called every hour.*

*Beginning at the Guard house which is Post No.1. the Guard will say Post No.1. 9 o'clock and all is well—no.2. will repeat the words and each guard in his turn until all have been heard from. If one fails to respond the relief guard is instantly sent out to see what is the matter. Last winter one of the guards was shot and killed with arrows which make no noise. Besides the danger from Indians is the danger from fire. We would be in sore straits if a fire should break out; with no adequate water supply and the river frozen over —*

*Dec 26. The winter is passing away. We have had little dinner dances and card parties to help pass the time. Some of the soldiers formed a theatrical troupe have an entertainment once a month. The one at Christmas was especially fine—Music dancing and a short play. Some of the men had Seen a good deal of acting and had probably done Some work on the board.*

*Dec 30 Last night the drum beat the alarm. A shot was fired in the vicinity of the Stables. After a long search Col Nugents's fat hog was found roaming around having been mistaken for an Indian. So we live in continual fear of attack—*

*Jan 1, 1868 Today the ladies of the Ft received. The officers came calling all in full uniforms. We made as much of a ceremony of it as we could.*

*April 15 The winter Seems very long we have read nearly all the books in the Ft. have read some of Dickens and Victor Hugo's.*

*April 25 We have spent the most of the day*

*Near Little Sandy Creek. Rick Greatz.*

on the river bank looking at the ice go out. The river is about half a mile wide and the ice breaks and comes down on a swift current, rushes pile up in great piles then on again tumbling and tossing constantly reminding me of "Barnaby's Dream" The ice was about 15 hours going out.

May 4 Lieut. C Started this morning with 25 mounted men to drive beef cattle to the mouth of the Mussle Shell where a summer camp, in tents, is to be established. . .I shall remain at the Ft. until a steam boat comes up and goes on to Ft. Benton and returns on the way to the States. One of the Ladies realizing how lonely she would be offered to board me if I would stay but if I cannot be with my husband I think I shall go home.

We have had great excitement to-day. About 3 P.M. Indians in great numbers were seen coming over the hills South of the Fort. They were about two miles away coming Straight to the Ft. The alarm was Sounded and soon every man was at his post at a loop hole. Our swivel gun in the bastion was manned and every arrangement was made for the defense of the Ft. The officers and ladies watched the coming of the Indians from the Sally-port. As they came nearer we Saw they were painted and mounted for war, having no women or children with them. They circled around three sides of the Ft., the river being on the fourth. The Commanding Officer took ten men and rode out to parley but was met by a volley of arrows and returned in hot haste. As soon as they were inside the Sally-port was closed. The Indians were so near that both Artillery and Infantry fire was opened on them which scattered them in short order. They made for the mountains rapidly as possible. We do not know their loss as each man is tied to his pony which will carry him away.

When the Ladies saw what might happen we held a "council of war" and decided if the Ft. could not be held that we preferred to be shot by our own officers rather than to be taken captive. The officers promised to do so before Surrendering—

May 30 Found the camp in an uproar. The Indians came in this morning killing two herders and driving off part of the beef cattle—The men will be buried at Sundown One Co. are out chasing the Indians. The Commander excused Mr. C from duty that he might visit with me but his sword and pistols are on the table and he may be called any minute as they are in a very hostile Section of the Indian country.

June 1, 1868 left camp at Sundown. It was a sad parting. The life at such a camp is So dangerous. I wanted to Stay but could not, and it will be so long before I get a letter—

Author's post script: Mr. Canfield joined Mrs. Canfield shortly after his resignation from the army in April 1869. After operating a store at Liscomb, Iowa, for a short time, he again taught school. In 1882, he received an appointment with the Pension Bureau in Washington, D.C. He attended night law school at Georgetown University, was graduated from the School of Law, and was subsequently admitted to the bar. In July 1905, Mr. Canfield died in Washington and was buried at Marshalltown. Mrs. Canfield, known as "Aunt Libbie" to her nieces and nephew, survived him by 27 years. She spent her last years at Marshalltown where she passed away September 4, 1932.

Mr. and Mrs. Canfield, however, live on. Their memories can be evoked by strolling around those remnants of Camp Cooke. With historian Harrison Lane our small group located the site of old Camp Cooke. We walked around the same area Mrs. Canfield walked over 100 years ago. Remnants of old moats were present as were mounds upon which the fort had been constructed. The bluffs on which she saw Indians also exist. To the south is the spot where Indians rode over the hill. In the same vicinity is the location of the most likely area Mr. Canfield and the troups engaged in battle. On a hot summer day, if one closes one's eyes, visions appear. One can hear the thunder of powder igniting a cannon and the slap of arrows striking the fort. But the slap is only the stirring of an excited beaver pounding its tail on the surface of the Judith River. The vision dies even harder when, digging through the dirt, we discovered the casing from an old Sharps Rifle.

# The Steamboat Era

For almost a century the Missouri River was the most important means of entry into the wilds that Lewis and Clark had explored. Up the river had come men, women, and families in virtually anything that would float. They came in bullboats, canoes, pirogues, bateaus, mackinaws, and finally keelboats.

The early crews that pulled these vessels upstream believed that steamboats could never ply such a treacherous river. Although they did, the resultant deaths were so common that they were recorded with a degree of nonchalance. A report on the sinking of one steamer in the mid 1800s stated, "Two sisters, large and fat, floated and were picked up by a skiff . . . another woman, thin and lean, sank and drowned."

But death could not prevent "manifest destiny." It could not quell the aggressive men and women who ventured west.

For decades the cry of "steamboat-a-comin'" had been heard along the Mississippi and lower portion of the Missouri. But only a few of these huge side-wheelers had ever attempted to navigate its upper reaches. Most sane people thought it impossible.

"The Missouri is too rough," said some.

"It is too fickle," said others.

"It is too much like a woman," implied another who then wrote: "Of all the variable things in creation, the most certain are the action of a jury, the same of a woman's mind, and the condition of the Missouri River."

But, in 1819, four steamboats left St. Louis bound for the mouth of the Yellowstone. The avowed purpose of the trip was to establish military posts and impress Indians with American power. Of the four comprising the fleet, one was wrecked, while two were discovered to be unfit for navigation on the Missouri. Only one reached a fort located below Council Bluffs in Nebraska.

Eleven years later, in 1830, The Yellowstone, built by Pierre Chouteau, managed to reach Fort Union. The steamboat was a small affair, only 130 feet long and 19 feet wide. It had a hold of six feet. Unlike most that would follow, this one was a side-wheeler. It had only one engine and, when it failed, the crew propelled the boat with poles. In subsequent years, The Yellowstone made many trips beyond Fort Union, but never to Fort McKenzie. That was a feat that remained for one of the Missouri's most intrepid of all steamboat captains.

*The steamboat DeSmet at Fort Benton in the 1870s.*
*Courtesy, Montana Historical Society.*

## Biggest Bang In The West

In 1859, The Chippewa left St. Louis for the upper Missouri. Her master was Captain John LaBarge, and one of the best steamboat men who ever navigated the Missouri. The destination was Fort McKenzie, located a few miles below Fort Benton. The group feared the boat would be unable to pass the Judith River because of shallow water. But, by removing some of the freight, this difficulty was overcome. The vessel floated higher, and the first steamboat reached Fort McKenzie on the 17th of June, 1859.

Several years later, The Chippewa would not fare so well. One risk in the steamboat trade was the engines themselves—they were exceedingly dangerous, since water and steam gauges were not yet in use. The inevitable result was that many steamboats were blown sky-high when excessive steam pressure ripped the seams of overworked boiler tanks. Wood fire heated these tanks adding to the hazard.

As The Chippewa landed at Poplar in 1861, passengers barely had time to rush ashore when smoke was noticed. From the safety of the shoreline, they watched the fire spread over the boat, finally reaching her cargo of gun powder. The resulting explosion created what must have been the West's biggest bang.

After the Civil War, sightings of steamboats on the upper Missouri became a common occurrence. There was, however, a difference in their appearance. These later boats were unpretentious, ungarnished, stern-wheel powered, and could carry 200 tons through waist-deep water.

Shallow-hulled and broad beamed, they were multi-tiered craft that could work their way over sand bars. They were "mountain boats," designed for use in Montana waters where the river grew increasingly threatening—particularly along the 130-some miles between Cow Island and Fort Benton. There the river bottom changed from soft sand to hard rock, and steamers entered a succession of 15 stretches of whitewater in which hulls were in continuous danger from sharp reefs and outcroppings. Little wonder steamboats were slow to appear in Montana's upper Missouri River.

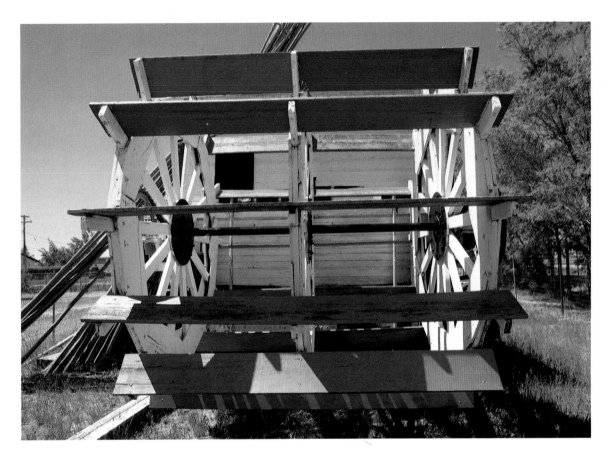

*Steamboat lore lives on in towns along the Missouri.*

*Top: A reconstructed sternwheeler at Poplar. Robert Gildart.*

*Left: "Bones" of an unlucky vessel at Fort Benton. Tim Church.*

*Above: Right: Relics on display at Fort Benton. Tim Church.*

## Innovative Navigational Techniques

To overcome the dangers of navigation on the Missouri, pilots had to memorize the locations of "Big Muddy's" endless bars, bends, and chutes. They had to be prepared to cope with the fickle nature of the Missouri, and, to do so, pilots mastered a variety of techniques.

One technique used to overcome an obstruction was sparring, or "grasshoppering." For this maneuver, the ends of two huge poles or spars were lowered forward to the bottom of the river at a 45-degree angle and fastened to the side of the boat. Cables attached to the upper part of the poles and to a capstan powered by an auxiliary engine pulled on the long timbers and moved them down and back, crutch-fashion, forcing the boat to slide a few yards ahead before the poles were robbed of their leverage by movement of the boat. This process was repeated until the steamer finally floated free in deeper water beyond the obstruction.

"Double tripping" was another method used. for the same purpose. To provide greater flotation, steamers unloaded all cargo, transported their passengers to their point of destination, then returned for the cargo. In 1869, a year of extremely low water, 18 of the 24 steamers which reached Fort Benton had to leave their cargo at Dauphin's Rapids, about 10 miles below Fort Benton.

Another technique used to negotiate rapids was to bury a heavy timber or "deadman" forward in the muck on the bank and, again, using the capstan with a hawser, to slowly inch the boat ahead.

As if the Missouri wasn't enough of a problem, captains of each vessel also had to be able to cope with the type of men who sought out employment on vessels where life seemed so cheap.

Crews were in three categories: steamboat mates, firemen, and roustabouts. Steamboat mates were charged with the task of extracting work from the roustabouts. Frequently the job required the use of fists and occasionally even clubs and guns.

Roustabouts were the work force of a steamer; they hauled the steamer over sandbars, off snags, and through freshly formed ice. They were the backbone of the operation, but they were also the most scorned of men. They came from a mix of ethnic minorities including blacks (considered most dependable) to Irish (considered least dependable). On call day and night, they were a motley crew that ate only after the passengers had been served. At the sound of their dinner bell, they would sink filthy hands into a communal "grubpile." It was first come first served.

Firemen had the best of duties. As they had to be alert every minute while on duty, their watches seldom exceeded several hours.

Passengers also faced hardships. Some of the lower paying ones were required to sleep amid cages of complaining cats, which were usually shipped upriver to combat rats that ate government grain faster than the horses at cavalry posts.

Some boats provided deck passengers with barrels of river water for drinking and washing to which prickly pears were added to "settle the mud." Other vessels simply offered the thirsty a bucket tied to the end of a long rope—a device that might yank the incautious overboard when lobbed into the stream beside a moving hull.

*Accommodations for the Missouri River traveler were rugged. Adding prickly pear to drinking water was thought to settle the mud. Phil Farnes.*

## Heroes

Pilots who plowed the Missouri River with their floating fireboxes were highly esteemed, and commanded special recognition. They lived before a time when the general public had become jaded by technology, and men of exceptional talent were still recognized as heroes.

Two such men to emerge as popular idols were Captain Joseph LaBarge and Captain Grant Marsh. Tough and aggressive, they could handle the roughest of men and situations. The exploits of these men abound in legends of the Missouri.

On June 6, 1862, LaBarge was on his way to Fort Benton when passengers of another steamer were treated to a few minutes of unexpected excitement.

A river race was in the making; LaBarge had accepted a challenge. Passengers of both vessels cheered on their respective crafts as the two steamboats pushed against the current, neck and neck, for more than a mile up a dangerously narrow channel. As the space between the boats diminished, The Spread Eagle tried to gain the lead. She swung into the path of LaBarge's Emile, his daughter's namesake. Unable to steer clear, she rammed La Barge's steamer. While watching timbers splintering on the starboard side of his vessel, La Barge swore a mighty French oath, grabbed a rifle and aimed it at the head of the other captain. LaBarge judiciously reconsidered his actions when he noticed the muzzles of several rifles pointing at him from the decks of The Spread Eagle. There was no shooting, but a passenger on the Emile noted in his diary that there was a good deal of angry talk. In St. Louis, La Barge's rival was charged with reckless behavior and, for a time, lost his license.

It was while traveling between Fort Union and Fort Benton that Captain Marsh earned much of his reputation as a leader capable of dealing with non-conforming and unwilling men. Later, he added distinction to his name when he ferried support troops up the Bighorn and, finally, to the mouth of the Little Bighorn. Here, he waited until the Crow scout, "Curley," brought the first news of the most publicized white military tragedy in the West. Custer had been wiped out! Hours later Marsh converted his steamer The Far West into a

Top: Steamboat Rock. Robert Gildart.

Bottom: Burned Butte, taken at LaBarge Rock. Jim Romo.

hospital ship which cared for the wounded men associated with Custer's defeat. Then, defying an unwritten rule prohibiting the navigation of steamers at night, he moved his hospital ship down perilous waters reaching Fort Lincoln in only 54 hours. It was a record never equaled.

## Steamboats, Cottonwoods and the River Today

Today's casual observer is unlikely to consider the ecological impact these wood-burning riverboats had on the surrounding area, but Montana biologist Ken Walcheck has done a thorough analysis. His research indicated that on a 67-day journey from St. Louis to Fort Benton The Shreveport stopped 71 times to take on 1,051 cords of wood. With costs averaging $15 per cord The Shreveport spent $6,048.70. Ken further discovered that between the years 1860 and 1888, 400 stern-wheelers operated on Montana's portion of the Missouri. He also found that: The average time to travel from the mouth of the Yellowstone to Fort Benton was about 23 days; 30 cords of wood were utilized a day; and 400 steamers smoked up about 276,000 cords. "And that," says Ken, "is enough wood to build 26,663 modern three-bedroom houses or fill a gargantuan woodbin holding 35,228,000 cubic feet." It is little wonder that the indigenous cottonwoods gradually ceased to lend grace and beauty to the banks of the Missouri.

Today, as we float along, we see that some cottonwood trees line the Missouri—at least mature ones. But, where are the young ones?

Near the Slaughter Creek Campground are dense groves of young cottonwoods, but this is one of the few areas where they abound and only because these trees are an experimental plot. Most of this land is state owned, and has not been disturbed for years. Cattle have not been permitted to enter the area, and it has remained free from floods. Consequently, the stands of trees reach as high as 15 feet.

Potential seedlings need disturbed sites—generally found in the flood plain—that must also be free from shade. Then once they have found a favorable spot for growth, they need to remain undisturbed for a few years. But such conditions are now rare along the Missouri, because of upstream dams.

Fluctuating water levels alter the environment required to create the refreshing groves of stately cottonwood. Jim Romo

The Missouri River near Floweree. John Reddy.

## The Fire Canoe

Indians called steamboats "fire canoes," and they initially stared in awe as the first "smoke-breathing" boats plied the upper Missouri. So-awed were Missouri River natives by the "drag-ons that walked on water" that, upon one's ap-proach, they frequently shot their horses and dogs to appease the Great Spirit. To them it was a living creature, and they said, "It sees its way and takes the deep water in the middle of the channel."

But by 1831, or a little more than a decade after the first steamer appeared, Indians were so ac-customed to the vessels—and the amenities they brought—that they paraded after them as they departed for downstream ports. Little did they realize in 1831 that from aboard these same boats would march a never ending series of plagues: cholera, venereal disease, small-pox, liquor, unscrupulous Indian agents, soldiers, guns and cannons.

One of the first, of the plagues was fire water; the white traders, most effective bartering com-modity. But alcohol induced both drunkenness and hostility, the latter increasing after 1860, this time in response to the influx of gold-hungry pro-spectors. And since many were coming via the Missouri, river traffic was hit particularly hard.

To destroy a steamer, Indians had to wait until the fire canoe either hit a sand bar or had to stop for wood. It was far easier for Indians to lay siege at points of known obstacles or at potential wood supplies that were manned by wood-hawks. In either case, the boat and her passengers were vulnerable.

If the attack came when a boat was grasshop-pering over a sand bar, the captain would send his passengers to the pilot house. This area was covered with boiler iron perforated with small peep holes. For further protection, all steamers carried howitzers.

## Woodhawks

Woodhawks led a desperate, almost suicidal existence, isolated in the prairie and river breaks among often hostile Indians who tried to deny them the sale of fuel to the boats. Later, the In-dians competed for this business and used rascal-ly treachery to lure it their way. Some dyed the ends of green logs to impart a look of age while others squatted up to their necks in shallow water to create an impression of depth to draw the boats aground and make them vulnerable to Indian depredations.

Thus the life of a woodhawker was filled with hardship and discouragement, as the journal of Kock, a Danish woodhawker working near the mouth of the Musselshell, confirms:

"Oct. 8. Twenty-five years old and poor as a rat. Cut down a tree on the cabin.

"10. Cutting while Joe is on guard. Snow tonight.

"24. Killed my first buffalo. He took 7 spencer and 6 pistol balls before he died. River full of ice.

"Nov. 25. Fred and Olsen started out wolfing. We stopped chopping on account of shooting and shouting in the hills. Joe and I found 4 wolves at our baits.

"Dec. 10. Sick yet. Bill, Joe and Mills went to Musselshell, said Indians had attacked and stolen 3 horses and mule but lost one man.

"24. Christmas eve. No wolves.

"Jan. 16. Awful cold. Froze my ear.

"Jan. 17. Too cold to work. Went to Musselshell. Froze my nose.

"Apr. 24. Sixty Crows went up the river after Sioux to avenge the killing of 29 Crows. They were all looking dreadful, had their hair cut off, their fingers and faces cut, with the blood left on their faces.

"May 9. One hundred and seventy cords on the bank. We put fire to the brush piles. The fire spread and burnt up 50 cords. We were played out before we got it checked. Nothing to eat.

"24. Raining. The 'Ida Reese' passed about daybreak without our knowing it.

"28. Sold 'Deerlodge' about 10 cords of wood.

"June 16. The 'Ida Stockade' passed without stopping. We took 6 cords back from the bank to keep it from falling into the river.

"July 4. Indians firing at us from nearest cot-tonwood trees . . . We went out and found one young warrior killed by a shot through the upper thigh. We got his gun, bow and arrows and two butcher knives and threw his body in the river. Waring scalped him."

Shortly thereafter Kock gave up and headed toward the Big Belt Mountains where he became an Indian trader and eventually a director of Bozeman's First National Bank.

Not all woodhawkers permitted the Indians to drive them out. Some became more savage and resourceful in the ways of the wild than the In-dians themselves. One such Missouri River man also working near the Musselshell was "Liver Eating Johnson." Johnson came up the river in 1843 and after a Crow war party invaded his cabin and murdered his Flathead Indian wife, he began killing, scalping and eating the liver of his Indian victims—most notably the Crow. Many of his contemporaries were repulsed. Still, they argued as to whether he "chewed the raw livers down, only spitting out the gristle," or whether he "simply made gobbling sounds while rubbing

*Above: Cow Island is a landmark of the middle Missouri and a historic crossing point. Rick Graetz*
*Right: UL Bend often offered travelers their first chance to walk on terra firma after weeks of steamboat confinement. The narrow peninsula was usually safe for a stroll. Robert Gildart.*

the bloody mementos in his whiskers."

Passengers had it no easier than did the soldiers and members of the crew. The diary of John Napton describes this trip and tells of privation, death at the hands of Indians, and death from inattention.

## Journey on the Imperial

John Napton spent the winter of 1866-67 in Bear Gulch, Montana, and, having made what he considered a stake, decided it was time to return to civilization. Traveling down through Prickly Pear Canyon, Napton reached Fort Benton several days later.

According to Napton's journal, three boats were tied up to the bank of the river, one of which was the Benton. The Imperial, according to his log, was at Cow Island, about 100 miles below, and had not been able to reach Ft. Benton because of low water. Agents of The Imperial, however, were there in full force and represented their boat as a floating palace. Napton found The Imperial and described it as "a large stern-wheel boat, but not very palatial in appearance." Said Napton, "They had secured about 275 passengers and had accommodations for about half that number. At night the whole cabin was filled with men rolled up in their blankets as thick as sardines in a box." For the privilege of traveling aboard this steamer, Napton paid the captain $130 in gold dust.

"Although we made slow progress from the start," wrote Napton, "I never saw a happier, jollier crowd...Here was truly a paradise for game. Small herds of buffalo could be seen at a distance on the prairies, and in the bottoms along the river, elk and white-tailed deer were as thick as rabbits. Rocky Mountain sheep appeared constantly on the bluffs and bear tracks of almost any size were found along the river banks. The bears along here must have been as plentiful as in the time of Lewis and Clark. Everything gave promise of a prosperous and pleasant trip, but we had bad luck from the start and it stayed with us throughout the journey."

A pulley broke which badly lacerated and broke the leg of a deck hand. "There was no doctor on board," wrote Napton, "the leg was set in rough way, splints bound on, and the best treatment possible given, but the man gradually grew worse, and sometime afterwards died.

"At first we only used the spars in prying off a bar and if that failed, the mate would order if possible a dead-man planted on the bank, then a hawser would be stretched from the nigger to the dead-man and the pulling commence. The deadman was nothing more than a big cottonwood log, buried about 4 feet in the bank, and the capstan in the vernacular of the deck hands was called the nigger. If this failed to move the boat, the Captain would call for volunteers from the passengers and boat crew to get in the water, about three on each side of the boat, and drag a long chain back and forth under the boat to start the sand moving. This worked well, but the water was too cold, and this plan had to be abandoned.

"Later it was decided all should leave the boat and pull on the hawser stretcher from the boat to the land. Two hundred men pulled together . . . we were making little headway, some days four or five miles a day, sometimes forty-eight hours on the same bar and as a last resort we concluded to cut away the upper deck of the boat and cache all the freight which consisted of bales of furs and buffalo hides stowed in the hold of the boat."

Several days later The Imperial encountered an immense herd of buffalo. This broke the monotony of life on board, and everybody was eager for the chase. Both yawls soon were filled with men on their way downriver. Several, according to Napton's journal, who could find no place in the yawls concluded to go by land. Among them were S---- and his partner Arnold.

S---- was a noted hunter and had been hired by the Captain at Fort Benton to hunt for the boat whenever a chance occurred. After going only a short distance, S---- separated from Arnold and started off by himself, but finding the trail indistinct and brushy, concluded to return. Near the spot where he left Arnold, searchers found Arnold lying in the path full of arrows, scalped and horribly mutilated . . . In the morning about twenty men well armed went to bring in the body. They found one bloody moccasin but saw no Indians.

"We buried him the next day at the foot of a large cottonwood and here must have been a favorite burning place for the Indians as several dead Indians were seen in the trees near by and a great many bones in all stages of decay were scattered around. Arnold was from Georgia."

According to Napton's recollections The Imperial reached Fort Buford in the latter part of October, where the boat began making "slower progress than ever." With winter moving in, its progress placed them in a serious position. Spying a partially submerged mackinaw, he and several passengers left The Imperial and dug it out of the mud. Then they began their own journey down the river.

"There are are twelve of us in the mackinaw and four of us worked at the oars all the time. We traveled all day and all night when not too dark, and estimated we made from fifty to seventy-five miles every day and one day when the wind was favorable we hoisted our blankets for sails and we thought we made fully a hundred miles.

"We soon reached Yankton and there hired horse wagons to take us to Sioux City. From Sioux City we took a stage to some point in Iowa; then on to St. Jo, Kansas City and arrived at Booneville, Missouri, where my cousin Lewis lived, exactly three months to a day from the time we left Bear Gulch, Montana.

"Some time after reaching home I saw a notice in the then Missouri Republican stating that the steamboat Imperial had been abandoned in the Upper Missouri River about a hundred and fifty miles above Sioux City and the passengers were all safe and were being transported to Yankton in horse wagons." John Napton, Westfall, Oregon, Nov. 8, 1915.

Many who made the trip up the Missouri—most with less difficulty—would look back as did Napton. They would look for old journals, letters, and misplaced diaries, so that they might relive their moments of adventure into Montana Territory. Many would speak of the grandeur of the region. They were some of the first and the last to see the Missouri when vast herds of buffalo churned waters surrounding a boat to a frothy chocolate and to watch as Audubon sheep cavorted from spire to spire.

But scenes of visionary enchantment still exist; scenes unaltered by the passage of time. Here and there are days when the late afternoon sun colors cliffs of Eagle Sandstone from crimson red to faint pink. And there are moments yet when sheep are cavorting from cliff to cliff and the sky is dotted with hundreds of white pelicans. These creatures sparkle like glistening diamonds thrown high into the sky overhead. On days like this we realize why men were lured to the banks of the Big Muddy — and why they still are.

# River Towns

Top: Fort Benton c. 1937. Courtesy, Montana Historical Society.
Bottom: Artist's conception of Fort Benton during the Steamboat Era. Courtesy, Montana Historical Society.

## ABANDONED TOWNS

There were never many people involved in the activities along our frontier river. In 1870, 177 inhabitants were tallied living by the Missouri River from "Fort Benton to the line." These included only one white female. The occupations listed were: Indian trader, trapper, hunter, saloon keeper, gunsmith, woodchopper, teamster, steamboat engineer, river pilot, clerk, and bookkeeper. A note at the bottom of the handwritten census page certifies the hazards of living in forbidden country: "16 scalped by Indians last year and left for dead. Well and hearty now. Hate Indians." A further description concluded: "There is not an acre of farming land cultivated . . . no one raising stock . . . the country is unorganized . . . no local government. Vast number of buffalo, elk, deer, antelope, mountain sheep, bear and other game abound. Indians are jealous of encroachments for they claim it as a favorite hunting ground."

This was the Missouri River below the Great Falls in 1870 with its transient towns, most of which survived for only brief periods of time. During their heyday, they were some of the roughest and most lawless areas the West had ever seen. Each of the towns were proud of their worst periods, and many claimed for one reason or another to have been the most corrupt.

Unlike Fort Benton and Great Falls, which also built their early histories on lawless activities, most lacked the advantage of being located at strategic points, and either died with but brief spasmodic kicks or carried on until today as slumbering outposts, waiting for the return of a forgotten era or the creation of a new revolution.

And the towns that died? Some left behind ghosts, and they lurk yet along the Missouri.

## Ophir & Carroll

With the advent of steamboat travel, a number of sites began competing for trade. One such place was the town of Ophir. Like the evolving Fort Benton, Ophir was located near the Marias River.

In the late 1850s, the Ophir Townsite Company surveyed for the prospective town and offered lots for sale. A steam sawmill was purchased, and men were sent out to obtain logs in preparation to building. Ten men in a logging crew were surprised by a band of Blackfeet Indians and all were massacred and scalped. Thus ended the hopes for the town of Ophir before it was born.

But the steamboats and trading established a need for additional locations along the river, and the long-empty space between Fort Union and Fort Benton began to fill in.

In 1874 one more attempt to undermine Fort Benton's success was made. The Diamond R Transportation Company sought government help to survey a southern trail from a point on the Missouri's south bank above the ill-fated mouth of the Musselshell through the Judith Basin and on to Helena. The company proposed to construct a town on this bank of the river and to name it Carroll, after one of the Diamond R partners, Mathew Carroll. The Northern Pacific Railroad had reached Bismarck, North Dakota, and with steamboat transportation to Carroll and freightline from there, the river season would be longer and the entire time to the gold camps shorter. The settlement of Carroll was built, and the army made plans to protect the Carroll Trail on its hazardous crossing of unsettled Indian country. Eventually, high water caused most steamers to pass up the Carroll site in favor of Fort Benton. Still, Carroll persisted as a trading post, but its ambitions as a river port were doomed.

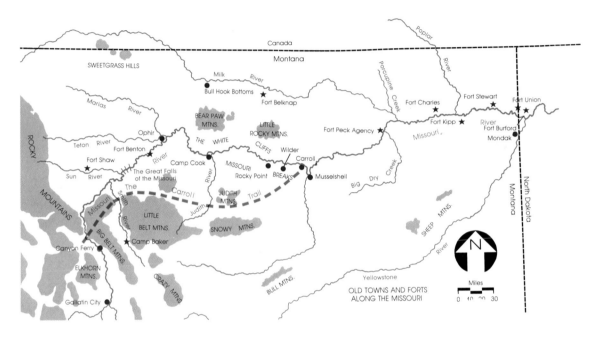

OLD TOWNS AND FORTS ALONG THE MISSOURI

## Inception of Rocky Point

Above Carroll, there had long been a site for loading and unloading supplies. This area grew and became known as Rocky Point, with a settlement of a dozen or more buildings. In 1881, business at Carroll deferred to that at Rocky Point—a town that was always on the raw edge of law and order.

One Rocky Point patriarch was Milton Frederick Marsh. Marsh had come up the Missouri on the steamboat General Terry, and one of the first structures he built was a saloon. It was said that Marsh's rule was that "anything goes in his place except him and his back-bar mirror." To keep his customers' guns engaged with the least amount of harm, there was a tradition that a whiskey glass be placed on the end of the bar and anyone who wished could shoot at it. If they missed, the drinks were on them. If they hit, it was on the house. There is never any mention of Marsh using a gun or displaying one except when hunting.

*Five ranges of mountains can be seen along the Missouri. Shown here are the Bear Paws from across the Missouri breaks. Jim Romo.*

The life of this lawless frontier community revolved around Marsh and his place of business. Braver than most, he brought his wife and young daughter out to this rugged post; the only white women on that part of the river. Marsh provided Fort Benton with news of his domain, and, in later years, his daughter wrote down memories of her life as a child:

"While we lived at Rocky Point, Indians wore paint one morning. A lone Indian rode into town. Most of the men were a few miles up the river putting up hay on the bottom where the Robinson bridge now spans the Missouri River. My friend the little half-breed boy sensed possible trouble and held a gun on this Indian until we could get into a boat and cross the river to go up and get Daddy and the other men. At this time the Indians were having trouble at the Black Hills, but he had gotten away from the tribe and was on his way to the reservation. My father and the other men sat up all night on guard, but nothing happened. The next day about 25 tepees were pitched back of our house.

"Not knowing what might happen, we telegraphed Fort Maginnis and asked them to send troops. When they came the officer in charge sent for the chief and an interpreter. After some words the chief called the officer a 'white dog'. The interpreter refused to tell what the chief called the captain. I was standing by my father. I could talk Cree and I said, 'He isn't telling the truth. He called the captain a white dog'. In a few seconds things were happening. They ordered the Indians across the river. Those that could not get on the ferry boat swam across the Missouri with their travois and horses and were taken to Fort Belknap Agency."

The winter of 1886-87 was one of the most disastrous ever known by the stockmen of the Northwest. Many were put out of business and only a few, including Marsh, survived. Conditions in Marsh's area are reflected in a February 1887 item in the Fort Benton newspaper.

"John Hancock, an old timer well-known along the river, arrived from Rocky Point last night, having made the entire trip up the river with a sled drawn by a mule. He was seven days making the trip. He said to your Correspondent: 'The snow in the vicinity of Rocky Point is three feet deep on the level. In addition to a detachment of soldiers under Lt. H.S. Foster, 20th Infantry, there are about 120 people wintering there. The

*Abandoned homestead near Rocky Point. Robert Gildart.*

store, two saloons and an eating house are doing a brisk business. Cowboys are stationed along the river from Carroll as far as the Kuntz place. I saw only a few dead cattle; some of them have fallen over the bank of the river and were too weak to get up. Stockmen are reticent as to what they have seen on the ranges and nothing can be said about the actual losses of cattle until the snow disappears... hardest winter ever experienced in Montana'."

One colorful visitor to Rocky Point was a Pony Express rider named Powell (Pike) Landusky, a colorful individual who lived every phase of the river adventure to the hilt. Hailing from Pike County, Missouri, he came to the Montana river country as a boy in 1868 on the steamer Henry Adkins and was said to have created trouble enroute.

Trouble was Pike's way of life. He was invariably ready for a fight and always seemed to hold his own, regardless of the opponent's size—until he met another man who frequented Rocky Point.

That man's name was Kid Curry, and he was known to Milton Marsh. In Marsh's later years he

related what he knew of the violent confrontation that eventually occurred between "Kid" Curry and "Pike" Landusky. The story was told to Al J. Noyes, author of *In the land of the Chinook—The Story of Blaine Country*.

According to excerpts from the book, the Kid had become involved in trouble and arrested. For some reason he was placed in the custody of Landusky. Landusky remarked that he now had the Kid where he had long wanted him, and was not at all particular in the choice of language used in addressing him. He also fastened the Kid to a chain "for safe keeping."

According to Noyes, "After the Kid had come back from Benton he told several he intended to lick Landusky for the insulting remarks, made by Landusky—remarks that took into consideration the chastity of his mother and which no self-respecting man could possibly allow to be addressed to him without trying to punish the person who made them.

"In fact, he had told Pike that when he returned he would surely take revenge. Pike, after his return, tried to make friends, but the wound was so deep that nothing he could say could possibly pacify his enemy. Jim Thornhill tried to keep the Kid away as he was sure of the final results, that is, that one or the other would be killed."

The day of the tragedy came when the Kid walked into Jew Jake's saloon. Pike was drinking with his friends. Kid Curry explained what he was there for and, handing his gun to Thornhill, began to beat Landusky with his fists. At last Pike cried, "Enough." Then he took a handkerchief from his pocket to wipe the blood from his face. But simultaneously he pulled a revolver from his pocket. But the pistol failed Pike. Had it not, as Noyes writes, "the Kid would have led the procession to the lonely grave on the south slope of the Rockies instead of Pike."

But the Kid's companion saved him. Thornhill saw the movement and shouted: "Look out, Kid, he's going to shoot!" At this Curry jumped and grabbed his gun which was held out to him by Thornhill and Pike fell shot to death.

Noyes writes that "If Curry had given himself up, he would—so most think—have been discharged, as Thornhill, who was arrested and tried for complicity, or as an accessory, received no sentence. Curry, however, seemed to fear jail and imprisonment. He was never captured and he became an outlaw."

The rest of the story about the Kid has been told in other books and has been the subject of material for movies. Kid Curry became a train robber and is thought to have been the ringleader in a Great Northern train robbery that took place near Wagner, a town north of the river country. The Kid eventually became the object of search by every lawman and Pinkerton from Canada to Mexico, but he disappeared. The rough country of the Missouri River provided his cover, and he vanished into the breaks, somewhere near Rocky Point.

## Stranglers of Rocky Point

The dilapidated cabins of Rocky Point are all that remain of the once turbulent era of men who operated there. And, not too much is left of them. Walk into one of the buildings, push open a door, and a shower of dust greets the visitor. Above is a series of gnarled rafters. They are high enough to throw a hangman's rope over and to place a box underneath a man's feet leaving space for him to fall after the box has been kicked away.

Outside the buildings there are a few cotton-wood trees. Under one of these monarchs it is easy to imagine the sounds of a scuffle. Then a band of men appears. A noose flips over a short branch and slowly the unfortunate one is hauled up. No kicking box is needed, if one is not too concerned about the swiftness of death, even though his dying request may have been, "Just give me a clean drop."

Many such hangings were committed in the area, and today, whether the vigilantes were justified in their actions no one can say. All that can be said with any degree of fairness is in a lawless country, it was time for citizens to take the law into their own hands. In the period following the Civil War, the Missouri River country had evolved into an intensely lawless place.

The introduction of stock precipitated much of the illegal activities. During the summer of 1880, a few herds of cattle were trailed into the Missouri River country. Here, they were turned loose to feed on the lush vegetation that grew along the river bottoms.

As time went by, more cattle were brought in and with them came cattle rustlers, horse thieves, and other desperados. A number of these characters began selling whiskey to the Indians, an act that increased cattle depredations and further inflamed the ire of cattlemen. The time was

ripe for a hanging. Maybe more than one! Arriving at Fort Maginnis above the mouth of Dupuyer Creek, about 30 miles south of Rocky Point, half-breed Sam McKinzie provided the first excuse.

Sam was caught riding a stolen horse. A group of cowboys from a nearby ranch recognized the horse and the rider. Sam was also known to have helped drive stolen horses across the line into Canada. Locking him in jail for the night, the next morning the group of self-appointed lawmen took Sam to a cottonwood tree and hoisted him by a rope into eternity. Sam did not get a "clean drop." From this episode these vigilantes received the name "stranglers."

In the years that followed, the stranglers became a very effective force in eliminating outlaws from the Missouri country. Occasionally, they didn't get the right man, but perhaps that was immaterial as it was alleged that those they mistakenly hung had most certainly committed a crime somewhere during their travels in the West.

Rocky Point became a meeting point for the stranglers. The shanty town was ideally situated. The group could ride in almost any direction and encounter outlaws. One time, not far from their headquarters, a group of stranglers encountered two men who were running a woodyard as a blind for their horse-stealing activities. The vigilantes came to their cabin at night and hanged Sam LaFevor and Charley Gibbs from the ridgepole inside the cabin. The next day, on their way downriver, they met Frank Belwaux who was on his way to Rocky Point. Frank did not reach his destination; he had boasted a little too loudly of his dishonest deeds.

Efficiency may have been one of the operational guidelines of the Missouri River stranglers. Recognizing that they needed help, they once decided to spare a man's life in exchange for information concerning the whereabouts of his companions. "Flopping Bill" not only agreed to locate his companions for the stranglers, he also helped hang them. "Red" Brocky Gallagher and Mike all met their maker at the mouth of the Musselshell, a major tributary of the Missouri.

Outlaw camps originally extended at intervals along the river bottomlands of the Missouri as far as Wolf Point. But when the stranglers were through, few outlaws were left. Some abandoned the country, and others drifted into obscurity with the changing times.

## Mondak

The Snowden Bridge, located north of Glendive near the old town of Mondak, harbors one such specter. Built to accommodate both railroad and vehicular traffic, the bridge spans today's quiet, muddy Missouri. But once these waters must have run a turbulent crimson red.

The bridge and its legacy of death were linked with the last spasms of a dying town—one which many like to say was created by North Dakota prohibition and destroyed by nationwide prohibition. Called Mondak, because of its location in Montana and its proximity to North Dakota, it is three miles west of the present-day historic site of old Fort Buford.

Mondak, with 17 saloons, was strictly a liquor town where, early in the 20th century, North Dakotans could visit their neighboring state and quench their thirst. The permanent Mondak population of about 250 possessed the true frontier spirit; it behaved as one large family, defending each other against any stranger. But the transient population was different. About 800 to 1000 cowboys, tinhorn gamblers, and dudes regularly ventured into Mondak. Mondak saloons averaged between $50,000 to $80,000 a year in liquor bought from St. Paul breweries, and three other wholesale breweries further supplemented the supply. The highest liquor expenditure for one year was reportedly $150,000!

A red light district of 15 houses lay between the town and the Missouri River. Since many of the killings occurred there, gunmen made a profitable business by furnishing protection to customers of the district.

In the murky backrooms and saloons, gambling stakes were high. In Mondak, $15,000 to $20,000 often changed hands in one night. A little farther west, Plentywood, Montana, boasted exchanges of $50,000 to $60,000.

There was a killing, either a shooting or a knifing, almost every night in Mondak. Each evening the seeds of hostility were planted. In the morning, the undertaker harvested a new crop of bodies.

Cowboys would shoot up the town when they returned from the range. They shot the bottles on the saloon shelves, roped the wooden lamp posts and dragged them down the street, and otherwise thoroughly frightened the inhabitants of the town. One area banker admitted that he hid in his walk-in vault for safety at such a time.

Few of the fights, knifings and shootings received much publicity. But, the murders of April 4, 1913, and a subsequent lynching still survive in the minds of local residents.

At the time, the Snowden railroad bridge was under construction several miles west of Mondak. One of the laborers, J.C. Collins, a black man, was wanted in the South for questioning in regard to an unsolved murder.

The flyer bearing the charge and his description was nestled in the pocket of Tom Courtney, newly elected sheriff of Plentywood. Ordering Burmeister, his deputy, to accompany him, Courtney headed for Mondak.

In town, the sheriff deputized Ted Wilson, a citizen, to guide the lawmen to the bridge construction camp on the Missouri River. The three sent Wilson to the office of the Union Bridge and Construction Company to determine the whereabouts of Collins. Fortunately for Collins, it was he who answered Wilson's query.

According to an old newspaper account, Collins rasped, "Looking for me?" From his belt he pulled an automatic pistol and disarmed Wilson. Then Collins walked out of the office door. Calmly, he stopped there and, taking deliberate aim, shot Sheriff Courtney and Deputy Burmeister. Collecting their weapons, he made a fast break for the woods surrounding the camp.

What chaos must have followed! One man, the sheriff, had been killed instantly; the other had been horribly wounded, shot once through the body, once in the shoulder and twice in the knee.

Collins ran, but the weather was not in his favor. It was Friday, April 4, 1913, and the ice on the Missouri was breaking up. That barred an escape route to the south. And the thin woods in all other directions offered no real refuge. Already, armed men in the woods were there searching for him. He had no place to go.

Collins must have known that death awaited him should he surrender. But he apparently didn't give enough credit to the brutality of a search party reacting to his own violent act and he made a fateful decision to turn himself in.

One can only wonder if utter fatigue had not impaired his thinking. With desperate fear he hobbled into camp hoping, perhaps, for a trial, speedy execution and a decent burial.

At first it may have seemed to Collins that he

made the right decision. His surprised captors handcuffed the killer and then loaded him aboard a wagon for the trip to the Mondak jail. Here, guards found they had their hands full protecting the prisoner from irate workers who would have hanged him on the spot. A guard of citizens and men from the bridge were posted around the jail that night.

From Plentywood, Montana, came word that a mob of men, enraged by the murder, was heading for Mondak to take justice into their own hands. Some of the workers at the Snowden Bridge were equally anxious to take action, and a group of men soon gathered who had blood in their eyes. Milling outside, they waited for news of the badly wounded Burmeister.

At 9 o'clock the deputy died and the guards, sensing the nature of the mob, quietly disappeared. Soon, faceless, nameless men replaced the guards, entered the jail and grabbed Collins. Moments later they strung him up from a nearby telephone pole. The urgency of the hanging may have been initiated in part by a rumor that a local militia company was on its way to protect Mondak and its prisoner from the 200 blacks employed on the Snowden Bridge. But what became of the body?

*Local residents still believe the abutments of Snowden Bridge may encase the remains of a man lynched one bleak evening in 1913. Jim Romo.*

## TOWNS THAT ENDURED

## Fort Benton

Fort Benton was one tough place, no question about it. And, even today, the town's residents are well acquainted with its lively history. Walk into the Overland Bar, have a seat, and before long, some oldtimer wearing weathered boots, a broken-down hat and faded jeans will belly up to the bar and begin reciting segments of the town's past. Selections will depend on his assessment of the listener.

"Yes sir," begins one local historian, "back in eighteen-hundred and sixty-eight, we had a sheriff here by the name of William Hinson. The man had come from Helena where he'd been charged with murder—as well he should have been. But he was acquitted. It was his powerfully persuasive tongue that helped him in Helena, and that must have helped him out here. At any rate, before long citizens of Benton found themselves with a new marshall. But soon our good people started to regret their decision. Before long citizens who may have had a bit too much to drink woke to find themselves without a single penny in their pockets. They'd been fleeced!

"Well, the marshall denied any knowledge of these activities. In fact, he made an announcement to the citizens of Fort Benton. Said the marshall, 'What our town needs is half a dozen hangings.' Several nights later the townfolks planted a man who feigned drunkedness and allowed the marshall to fleece him.

"Next day citizens of Benton showed up and announced to Marshall Hinson that they knew who had been stealing money from innocent drunks and would he help out by securing some rope, that they were going to hang the culprit in a half hour.

"Quicker than a man could say "scat," Hinton purchased some hemp and showed up at the hanging site. Then, before the unsuspecting marshall could escape, the local gathering hanged him with his own rope. Now that's the gospel."

Historical documentation bears out the raconteur. Paul Sharp has the same account in his book *Whoop-Up Country*, and many in Fort Benton seem to have read it and know what subsequently happened near the location of today's Episcopal Church. There Sheriff Hinson was hanged, just as another infamous Benton sheriff by the name of Henry Plummer should have been hanged before his career in Virgina City.

According to Fort Benton citizen Joel Overholser, a retired newspaperman and noted western historian, the hanging was just one of the many events that helped make Fort Benton one of the toughest towns in the West, and its history is relatively recent. So recent, in fact, that there are some things that a few of its residents still refuse to discuss. Some, according to a speaker addressing the Montana Historical Association in 1982, shy away from talk concerning the whiskey era and wolf trapping days.

Joel Overholser has encountered the same silence. "There are several men here I tried to pry information from for years, but they were closed mouth on certain subjects. Unfortunately, they are now deceased."

But according to Overholser, most of the town's history has been documented and he should know, for he's been amassing much of it himself. Taking bits of information from all over the state, he now has a good picture of what the area was like as it grew, prospered, and almost died—but then prospered once again.

The Benton Record, predecessor to Overholser's River Press (still operated by the family), is one paper Overholser relies on. According to a turn-of-the-century clipping concerning his town, it was a "squaw town, a scalp market, the home of cutthroats and horse thieves. The military denounced it as an ammunition depot and whiskey trading post for hostile Indians." Armed robbery, a lynching, or a gun-fight was expected daily, a fact of which some of the folks were downright proud. These people thrived on excitement. On record is the fact that when Mike Welsh, a local saloonkeeper, opened his joint one morning without finding the usual "stiff" sprawled outside with a bullet in his brain, he said: "I'm hitting the trail further west. This dump is getting too civilized."

Few, if any, towns in the Far West possess such a diverse and unique history as the town of Fort

*Fort Benton was the origination point of the "Whoop-Up Trail," which transported goods to Canada. Tim Church.*

Benton. It is one of the oldest settlements for trappers who began visiting the area as early as 1831. One historian wrote: "[Fort Benton] saw more of romance, tragedy, and vigorous life than many a city a hundred times its size and ten times its age."

Fort Benton grew in importance because of its location as the head of navigation on the Missouri River. But this was not the reason the fort originally became a settlement. The area had been known since the Lewis and Clark Expedition as one rich in furs, and free trappers and fur companies turned to it after having tried without success to tap the rich beaver streams of the northern Rockies. The mountain men who ranged the great West called the area bordering the upper Missouri River "Bad Medicine." And not without reason, for such intrepid trappers as "Bad Hand" Fitzpatrick, Jim Bridger, John Colter, Jed Smith, and Kit Carson had all learned to keep their distance from the hostile Blackfeet.

*At Fort Benton. John Reddy.*

## Virgelle

Virgelle never was a thriving town and it certainly isn't now. In fact the town's main resident, Don Sorensen, when not working as a relief pharmacist, operates a lone antique business in the old Virgelle Mercantile that was built to provide the ranchers and railroad workers with their supplies. Don's store is the only one that may be considered actively engaged in business in Virgelle. And, considering the isolated nature of the surrounding country, it is surprising that his business is there at all.

The sleepy town had its start when Virgil F. Blankenbaker came to Montana in 1886 and settled downstream from present Virgelle in 1889. Mr. Blankenbaker derived the town's name by combining his first name with that of his wife, Ella. During those early days, there were several other stores in the area, and each owner hoped to stimulate the building of a town. These stores and incipient towns were located about five or six miles apart along the river, and they competed fiercely for the business that was produced by the river traffic. But they could not survive, and, of the many, Virgelle is the last.

To reach Virgelle, one must drive down a winding dirt road that sometimes is transformed into a sea of gumbo by torrential rains that descend over the Missouri in the spring. If you're visiting the Merc in the winter you take a different chance, that of being snowbound as was Don in 1978. For seven days Don was isolated before plows could reach the store. Recalls Don, "The snow was 12 feet high in places, and the wind constantly kept the snow shifting back over the road."

But despite the remoteness of the area, Don still operates a profitable business in a store that first opened its doors in 1912. During those days there was a bank, which still exists, as well as a few homestead shacks that are being restored by Don for visitors who may wish to take advantage of another of his side-lines, a canoe catering service.

Don stumbled into the antique business in the early '70s while riding horseback on his father's

nearby ranch. Finding some old bottles, he took them back to the Merc and began lining the shelves. Many had contained laxatives. "Fifty to 60 years ago," says Don, "laxatives were a big thing. If you weren't regular, you were not considered healthy."

One of Don's prize possessions is an old pump organ. According to Don, it came up the Missouri on one of the last steamboats and was bought by his grandmother who later sold it for $12. It went through four additional sales. Eventually Don learned about the organ's family significance and bought it back. "To repurchase the organ," says Don, "required an expenditure of considerably more than $12!"

Today, many local people visit the Virgelle Merc. "But few," informs Don,"are really purchasing-type customers. Most come just to be reminded of the way things were about 100 years ago, not to purchase my antiques. These heirlooms are just too much of a reminder to them of the hard times they lived through."

*Top: The Missouri River Canoe Camp at Virgelle. Several outfitters along the river provide canoes and logistical support for floaters. Tim Lucas. Bottom: Virgelle Mercantile proprietor Don Sorensen. Robert Gildart.*

Steamboat traffic bolstered the growth of Fort Benton. Prior to that, transportation on the Missouri was carried on by a motley assortment of hand-propelled craft, including the canoe, mackinaw, bullboat and keelboat. But it was the mountain steamboat that encouraged and propelled the throng of humanity to their various destinies along the Big Muddy. In 1859, people on a voyage undertaken by Pierre Chouteau, captain of the steamboat Chippewa, reached the town. The next year, two steamboats reached Fort Benton.

On the two steamers were Major George A.H. Blake and 300 recruits on their way to the Pacific Northwest. Blake was to test the Mullan Wagon Road which was being constructed by the government to link the heads of navigation on the Columbia and Missouri rivers.

Gold lured adventurers up the Missouri after the decline of the fur era. In 1862, gold was discovered at Grasshopper Creek. In 1863 it was discovered at Alder Gulch and, in 1864, at Last Chance Gulch. Justifiably Fort Benton, as the major route to these areas, became known as the "Birth Place of Montana," "The Chicago of the Plains."

In 1865, supplies were reaching the mining camps of Montana by three different routes: overland via Salt Lake; over the Mullan Road by pack train from Portland and Walla Walla; and up the Missouri River from St. Louis to Fort Benton. Benton, as difficult as it was to reach, was the head of navigation. As was discovered during the trial and error period of the fur era, it was strategically located.

Initially the overland routes provided the most important link with Montana Territory. But after 1865, the improved construction of upriver steamers caused decreased reliance on the land routes and brought a marked increase in traffic on the upper Missouri. An additional factor that inhibited land travel was the virtual closing of the Bozeman Trail in 1866 by the hostile Sioux.

Traffic up the Missouri was in full steam in 1866. Thousands of miners had made the trip to Fort Benton sleeping in blankets on decks. Later, at Fort Benton, they were willing to pay any price for supplies, and this demand for merchandise caused ship traffic to skyrocket. Tobacco sold for its weight in gold. That same year 31 steamers discharged some 4,441 tons of freight at the Benton landing. Of this total, the Mollie Dozier carried 350 tons and the Peter Balen 334. Freight from the steamboats was stacked high on the open river banks, while muleskinners, bullwhackers and teamsters labored through the hot summer months to freight the merchandise to the mines. That same summer miners shipped two-and-one-half tons of gold dust from Fort Benton on the Luella. The next year, 10,000 miners took the river route to Montana.

Those involved with the tiny sternwheel steamers made fantastic profits. The entrepreneurs affiliated with the Peter Balen collected $100,000 for moving the goods from St. Louis. Owners of the steamer cleared $65,000, while its captain received $7,500 for piloting the vessel to Fort Benton. Renowned pilot of the Little Bighorn rescue mission, Captain Grant Marsh, received $1,200 a month for his trips up the Missouri.

Fort Benton attracted distinguished public servants as well as traders, sailors, and laborers. General Thomas Francis Meagher, acting governor of Montana could be counted as one of its most notable and sadly famous visitors. The governor is thought to have drowned there in 1867.

Meagher, a vitriolic Irishman had been a revolutionary in his home country during the 1848 uprising. Captured, he was sentenced to be hanged, drawn, and quartered. But he escaped and made his way to America where he served as a general of volunteers in the Civil War. At the end of the war Meagher's fortunes were so low that he needed a job at once. The post of Territorial Secretary in faraway, strange Montana was not much of a plum, but he took it as the best thing in sight and made the most of it as a challenge. In a letter to an old comrade, Captain W.F. Lyons, he said:

"It may be the last time (God only knows) that you shall see me, for I go to a fierce and frightful region of gorillas."

When Meagher arrived in Bannack he found the Territorial government contained in a log cabin. From the beginning, Meagher's rule was autocratic. First he quarreled with the Democrats, then with the Republicans. Then while under what Munson E. Lyman termed "his unfortunate habit," in his book Reminiscences, the acting governor granted a pardon to a man previously found guilty of murder.

Despite his authoritarian, and unpredictable disposition, Meagher was considered a compassionate man in his dealings with Indians. While serving as Territorial Superintendent of Indian Affairs, he visited Fort Benton to meet the Piegan Indians. During the course of his conference, a pile of choice buffalo robes was gathered nearby, each warrior contributing one. One of the Piegan chiefs announced in a speech to the governor that it was their custom, when visited by one of the "white fathers," to present a present as proof of their good will and esteem. They begged his acceptance of the buffalo robes and of a choice horse that had been sent for. Much to the surprise of the chief, the governor replied, "I thank you but cannot accept your presents. I am paid by the government for my services, and have no right to other compensations. You are poor and need your property; keep it for yourselves and for your children, who else may go cold and hungry in the coming winter."

Meagher's respect for the law and kindness to the Indians belied an Irish temperament, which may have caused his demise. To this day his untimely death has provided historians with much grist for the speculation mill. Whether the governor was mudered or drowned accidently has never been determined. An account by a prominent merchant, I.G. Baker, provides detail but no answer. According to Baker, the governor had been his dinner guest that fateful day of July 1. Later, the governor is said to have written a letter to his wife in Mr. Baker's office—the last that he ever penned to her. Then, growing restless, the governor decided to board a steamer docked at the levee for a round of cards.

On board, Meagher met some friends, and the evening was passed in a friendly manner, the governor drinking heartily. He became intoxicated, his temper flared, and he was offended by some unrecorded remark. He charged some of the men present with desiring to take his life.

The party finally broke up, and the governor retired. About ten o'clock in the evening, the pilot's watchman discovered a man struggling in the river and shouting for assistance. Within moments a number of people assembled on the shore opposite the scene of the occurrence. A boat was launched and a search instituted, but all in vain. The next summer word was received in Fort Benton that a body had been found in the Missouri, but it was never determined whether it was the unfortunate governor.

# Whiskey

Three years later, in 1871, the great gold rush came to an end and Fort Benton's population declined from 500 permanent residents to 180. Abandoned businesses included four Indian trading houses, a brewery, a bakers, and 12 saloons. The remaining residents were hungry for more business and began looking for new sources of revenue. Their search turned up the universal and powerful commodity: Whiskey! More precisely, Indian whiskey. The ingredients were simple and are recorded for posterity in the Fort Museum. Says the recipe:

"To muddy Missouri Water add 1 quart of alcohol, 1 pound of rank black chewing tobacco, 1 handful of read peppers, 1 bottle Jamaica giner, and 1 quart black molasses. Mix well and boil until strength is drawn from the tobacco and peppers." The concoction provided a lucrative revenue for almost one full decade until replaced by another source of wealth.

After a succession of deaths and near major battles, the whiskey trade was put out of business. One of the confrontations in Canada, the Battle of Cyprus Hills in Alberta was in part an outgrowth of the whiskey trade. Wrote Paul Sharp in Whoop-Up Country, "Whatever the truth about the Cypress Hills incident, its aftermath is clear. News of the fight aroused indignation throughout Canada...Though the (Canadian( government had already introduced a bill in Parliament to organize the Northwest Mounted Police, the news from the West reinforced the need for immediate action. Public clamor to end the whisky trade from Fort Benton..."

The mounted police brought law and order to Alberta and British Columbia and, stopped the flow of whisky into areas under its jurisdiction. Fort Benton needed a new source of revenue.

By 1879, as immigrant families moved through Fort Benton en route to Canada, merchandising in Benton began a recovery. Fort Benton again prospered just as it had during the "Golden Age" of the gold mining era.

# Benton's Papers

As Fort Benton became one of the permanent towns along the Missouri, it enticed three newspapers, only one of which still exists. The original owner of the current paper was the "Merchant Prince," T.C. Power, who sold it to Joel R. Overholser in the early '20s. Later, it was managed by his sons, Joel Jr. and Leland.

Today, at more than 80 years of age, Joel Jr. has relinquished management of the paper to relatives, but he still maintains an active interest in the area's history, publishing accounts of its bawdy background and conversing with the curious who pass through the town of Ft. Benton. Joel Overholser's fascination with the steamboat era and its influence on the town's past so influenced him that he became one of the state's most respected historians. He has also been active with the town's historical association and, with it, helped to upgrade Benton's informative museum and other historical landmarks. As a result, visitors can learn much of the tumultuous and fascinating history of the Missouri and Fort Benton by strolling the banks and streets adjacent to the river.

On the waterfront is an old keelboat like the ones that plied the Missouri along with steamers. The boat was used in the filming of the movie the "Big Sky." Also along the waterfront are the remains of the old steamboat and life-size, bronze statues of Lewis and Clark, Sacajawea and her infant son, Pompey, created by one of Montana's outstanding sculptors, Bob Scriver.

On Front Street is the Chouteau House, once a delux stopping place for travelers. Next door is an adobe house said to be the place Acting Governor Meagher ate his last meal before drowning in the Missouri. Continuing up Front Street one comes to the museum, rich with memorabilia.

But just as in former years, Fort Benton is for most adventurers the jumping off place for persons interested in floating the wild and scenic portion of the Missouri.

*Joel Overholser, Fort Benton Editor-Historian Emeritus. Robert Gildart.*

## Merchant Princes

Two merchants who feathered their nests from the commerce created by the Canadians were I.G. Baker and T.C. Power. Both of their companies thrived during the latter part of the 1860s and on into the early 1890s by building their businesses on the personnel and facilities left behind by the American Fur Company. And both companies relied on the Missouri, establishing offices in St. Louis from which point they would ship supplies north and west. Goods in the form of buffalo robes also continued to be shipped downstream from Fort Benton. According to records compiled by Joel Overholser, 445,000 buffalo robes were shipped between 1872 and 1882 alone. The companies prospered and used some of their earnings to improve the town.

The most spectacular building constructed during the time was the Grand Union Hotel, named, it is said, to commemorate the end of the Civil War. Designated as a historical site, it stands today as a sad but elegant building, struggling as ever to maintain financial integrity.

Construction of the hotel began in 1881 and required 15 months. There was a separate entrance and stairway for women and separate ladies' parlors so they would not have to encounter the rough frontiersmen who dominated other areas of the hotel.

*Below: Transported by steamboat up the Missouri and then by wagon to Virginia City, this historic back bar is still in use. Robert Gildart.*
*Right: Fort Benton's Grand Union Hotel once was the most elegant hostelry between Minneapolis and Seattle. Robert Gildart.*

## Thomas C. Power, 1839-1923

Thomas C. Power, born in Dubuque, Iowa, first entered Montana in 1864 as a civil engineer with a surveying party. He returned in 1867 to Fort Benton and opened a store stocked with merchandise he bought in St. Louis and brought up the Missouri by steamer.

Power traded with the Indians, the military, the itinerants and the white settlers. His post or trading establishments were scattered from Helena to Canada. With his brother, John, as a partner, the firm handled immense shipments of hides and furs for sale in the eastern markets.

In 1874, the Power brothers and I.G. Baker Company together purchased the steamboat Benton, the second of that name. This was the beginning of the Benton Transportation Company later known as the Benton Packet Company or "Block P." To the merchandise business the brothers added the steamboat company, freighting outfits, stage lines, banks, a large livestock business, and important real estate holdings in various Montana localities.

In 1890, Thomas C. Power was elected one of the first two senators to represent the new state of Montana in Congress. Power served from 1890-95. Until his death in 1923, T.C. Power managed the affairs of the firm which bore his name.

*Great Falls from Airport Hill. Lawrence Dodge.*

## Great Falls

The history of another enduring town on the Missouri dates back to the Lewis & Clark expedition. On Thursday, June 13th, 1805, Captain Lewis encountered the Great Falls of the Missouri. Of the occasion he wrote, "I had proceeded on this course about two miles... (when my) ears were saluted with the agreeable sound of a fall of water and advancing a little further I saw the spray arrise above the plain like a collumn of smoke which would frequently dispear again in an instant caused I presume by the wind which blew pretty hard from the S.W. I did not however lose my direction to this point which soon began to make a roaring too tremendious to be mistaken for any cause short of the great falls of the Missouri...

"I took my position on the top of some rocks about 20 feet high opposite the center of the falls...immediately at the cascade the river is about 300 yds. wide...the remaining part of about 200 yards on my right formes the grandest sight I ever beheld, the irregular and somewhat projecting rocks below receives the mater in it's passage down and brakes it into a perfect white foam which assume a thousand forms in a moment sometimes flying up in jets of sparkling foam to the hight of fifteen or twenty feet are scarcely formed before large roling bodies of the same beaten and foaming water is thrown over and concealks them."

Despite such early references to the Great Falls of the Missouri the area lay neglected until the

1880s. Fort Benton below and Sun River Crossing above had been settled by the 1860s. But the Great Falls area went unnoticed. It resources may well have remained unnoticed for years more but for the insights of one man, Paris Gibson.

Elaborating on his planned town Gibson wrote with regard to the falls near his preceived townsite, "In magnitude, the falls of the Missouri are unsurpassed in the United States except by the falls of Niagara. It is estimated that if all the power of Niagara could be harnessed, it would yield 1,000,000 horse power, while the available power at the Falls of the Missouri is placed at 350,000 horse power at a medium low stage of water. But while at Niagara, the fall is a single

56

Above: The Great Falls in harness. It's a popular picnicing area in the city. Ray Ozmon.
Right: Black Eagle Dam, one of 10 on Montana's portion of the Missouri that together generate 451.5 megawatts of power. John Reddy.

pitch of 150 feet, at the Falls of the Missouri there is a series of falls and rapids aggregating 512 feet. As it is hardly possible that engineering skill can ever devise a plan by which more than one-third of the power of the single pitch of the Niagara can be installed, it is safe to assume that the power of the Falls of the Missouri available for industrial progress is fully equal to that of the Niagara."

Gibson, who had suffered severe financial losses in Minnesota during the depression of 1873 came to Montana at the age of 49 to begin implementing new ideas. The year was 1879, and Gibson landed at Fort Benton, but soon was diverted to Great Falls by Captain Lewis' eloquent writing, which had stimulated his interest in the falls.

Over the course of several years, Gibson returned to the area and began evaluating it in terms of its water potential and lumber possibilities. He investigated the newly opened mines at Belt and Sand Coulee, which impressed him greatly.

In 1882, Gibson, along with several other men, drew up plans to erect a townsite adjacent to the Great Falls. Lacking financial backing, he contacted railroad magnate James J. Hill. Gibson's plans were so well conceived that Hill decided to back the enterprise. Mr. Gibson quickly began implementing his plan and, in 1887, the Great Falls Water Power and Townsite Company was incorporated.

The success of the settlement as Gibson had predicted depended on the advance of Hill's western railroad. It was a disappointment to Gibson and the new townspeople that Hill laid his road near the Canadian border. But Hill fulfilled his promise and constructed a branch line south to Great Falls. On October 15, 1887, Hill's St. Paul, Minneapolis and Manitoba Railroad chugged into the embryonic city.

Even before the first train arrived the city was vibrant with life and ideas. Under Gibson's direction a city with geometrically regular avenues began to appear. Within a few years the the town could boast of parks bordered with trees, industries and a library. From the beginning, Gibson was interested in building an orderly and beautiful city. It was incorporated on October 4, 1888, and Gibson became its first mayor. Today, the man's vision is manifested through schools and parks prefaced by the name Paris Gibson.

By 1890, the first dam on the Missouri, that at Black Eagle Falls, was completed.

*Giant Springs, the world's largest freshwater spring.*
*Ray Ozmon.*

*Opposite page: Top: Great Falls claims as part of its trade area a generous stretch of "Missouri Country." This is the town of Square Butte. Jim Romo.*
*Bottom: A gathering storm over wheat fields near Great Falls.*

Though the power the river generates may be the backbone of the city's economy, the river provides much in the way of aesthetics. On the downtown side of the Missouri, two miles of undeveloped land exists between Black Eagle and Rainbow falls. Between the two falls is Giant Spring. With 124,000 gallons per minute spewing·from underground it is the world's largest freshwater spring.

Great Falls also boasts of other parks. Over 40 recreation areas are contained within the boundaries of the city, most of which surround the city's many lakes and provide a diversion for people populating the states's second largest town. One ongoing project has been to develop the waterfront parks along the Missouri River.

Many of the Great Falls parks were designed for year-round use. Inner-tubes and sleds are a common sight at Overlook Park above the Missouri River while skaters eagerly await the freeze-over of a large pond in Gibson Park.

Because of the Missouri and the abundance of electric power generated by the five dams, the town acquired the name "Electric City."

With the growth of the Electric City came more industry. Included is one organization that has generated some controversy. Partially concealed by the endless rows of ripening grain are Minuteman II and III nuclear warheads—aimed at the Soviet Union.

Each year, on Easter Sunday, their presence draws anti-nuclear demonstraters to Malmstrom, the base responsible for the management of the warheads. But other than that particular day, there is little more in the way of negative comment, and with good reason.

With an unstable agricultural economy the city's residents and business people rely heavily on the base for an infusion of financial stimulation. And the money is there. According to a 1983 government financial report, the yearly economic impact of the base on Great Falls is over $257 million.

No discussion of Great falls would be complete without some mention of the city's—and states—most renowned artist, Charles Marion Russell.

Born on March 19, 1864, Russell traveled from his home in St. Louis at the age 16 to Montana. For the next 16 years, Russell was to work in various ranches throughout the state, attempting all the while to hone his artistic abilities, which he had expressed since a child. As he developed his talents, the owners of two of the Central Avenue bars, the Silver Dollar and the Mint, sold pictures for Russell. But it was 18-year-old Nancy Cooper, who married Charley when he was 32 and took over management of the business end of his work, who had the greatest influence on his success.

Charley died in Great Falls in 1926 leaving behind hundreds of works that remind us what the Missouri was like when grizzlies still fed on buffalo carcasses along the Missouri where dams are now seen. Perhaps no other artist captured the old west with the compassion, good humor and affection that Charles M. Russell had for his Missouri Country.

*Four free ferries operate on the Missouri. They are among a handfull left in the country, and are licensed by the U. S. Coast Guard. Photo credits from left: Jim Romo. Tim Lucas. Robert Gildart.*

## Ferry Towns

One honk of the car and out comes a man dressed in denim pants, shirt and hat. On the crest of the hat are grass seed pods, the awns of which have adhered to the hat making it appear they have been stuck there for weeks. This older man looks as though he has lived outdoors all his life which is not far from the truth.

He is Bob Otto—operator of the Virgelle Ferry. "So you want a ride," says Bob. "Well it won't cost you a penny. Free ferry, as the sign says, but you go at your own risk."

Bob Otto, like so many of the Missouri's colorful residents, is unique. He came to the Missouri River country rather late in life from Minnesota, where for six consecutive years floods wiped out Bob's wheat crop. Looking for something more stable, he gravitated west, landing a job along the Missouri at the PN Ferry, which he operated for 12 years until the recently constructed bridge put him out of work. As luck would have it, the death of another Missouri River operator provided him with another ferry—just a little farther upstream.

"Yup," says Bob. "A three and a half million dollar bridge put me out of work. Christ, for that kind of money other men and I could run a ferry a long long time."

During the operating season, Bob is furnished with a house, telephone and power. "But all that stops around Thanksgiving," says Bob. "Then we have to pay rent and live off whatever funds we can until the ice goes off the river. And that's generally sometime in April. Sometimes, my wife and I kill a deer or catch a few fish, and that helps."

Bob is subject to call 24 hours a day, and, during the summer, it's not uncommon at all to have to rise out of bed at three o'clock in the morning. "Ranchers," says Bob. "On weekends ranchers will go to Winifred and come back in the wee hours of the morning. And they're generally a little on the happy side. But, no, they've never given me any trouble. We get along pretty good. Hell, I just ride along with them on the ferry and drink one of their beers."

Upstream from Bob lives the busiest operator of them all, Ray Scheele, operator of the Loma Ferry. With his wife, Pam and their two children, Eric and Aaron, he puts in more than 80 hours a week or about 360 hours a month. In a typical year they will make well over 7,200 crossings.

As with most of the other four operators along the Missouri, their season begins about the 15th of March and runs until about the middle of November. During the off season Ray and his family move to either Fort Benton or Loma.

Some years the ferry boat season begins with snow on the ground, as in the spring of 1981. Ray reflects: "That year there was eight feet of ice on the river. To prepare an access for vehicles and the ferry, a Caterpillar was brought down. When the operator was finished we couldn't see the Cat; it was that bad. That same year, the temperatures had dipped to -54°F."

No year is ever the same along the Missouri, and it seems each year brings some unanticipated event that explains why the county posts a sign advising passengers that they must assume the risk for any accidents that may occur.

For the Scheeles, such an event occurred in August of 1983 when a young fellow drove a truckload of barley onto the ferry and failed to set his hand brake. When Scheele put the ferry into motion, the truck rolled off the end of the ferry and caused it to go under.

"For about 60 seconds," remembers Ray, "all we could do was watch helplessly as the ferry sunk, finally touching the bottom of the river, about seven feet down at this particular point. Out in the middle the river is 14 feet deep, so we

# River Ferries

*Right: Virgelle Ferry operator, Bob Otto. Robert Gildart.*
*Far Right: Loma Ferry operator, Ray Scheele. Robert Gildart*

were lucky it happened where it did.

"When the ferry finally did touch the bottom, I stepped onto the hood of the truck and went hand over hand on the cable to the shore."

To extricate the machinery Ray called for the services of a crawler tractor, which hooked the front end of the truck with a cable, turned the truck around and pulled in onshore. Next, they hooked the ferry and pulled it to the river bank. Says Ray, "It looks worse in the picture my wife took because the planks on the ferry are not attached. They have floated a little and that makes it look as though it has sunk deeper than what it really has and as though nothing could be salvaged. But the truck was still functional and within hours my ferry was back in operation. It is amazing no one was hurt. I felt so sorry for the kid, it was his first time to haul a load anywhere."

One of the most isolated ferry boat operators is Ken Gilmore, operator of the McClelland Ferry. Located south of Chinook and north of Winifred, the area frequently becomes a sea of gumbo. As a result Gilmore keeps a horse so that he can get in and out of the area. Once he was stranded for eight days.

Despite the isolation, Gilmore says he gets plenty of excitement, particularly when river floaters try to land on the upstream side of the beached ferry.

A few years ago a canoe carrying a man and a woman tried to dock upstream. "What they don't realize," said Gilmore, "is that the current flowing beneath the ferry increases to about 10-to 12-miles an hour."

Gilmore recalls that the man managed to scramble aboard the ferry, but that the woman and the canoe were sucked toward it. Other canoeists saved the woman when they scrambled aboard the ferry and caught her before she completely disappeared. But the canoe went under the ferry and then reemerged on the other side. "And," says Gilmore, "I'll never forget what happened next. The canoe shot out of there like a bullet. The canoe was O.K., and so was the girl. She was able to continue on her way down the Missouri, but water pressure had peeled the skin off her belly. And was she ever terrified!"

Another time two young men were floating down from the PN landing. One of them had been refining his quick draw skills with a .22 calibre pistol and wound up shooting himself in the leg. "I've seen enough bullet wounds," says Gilmore, "to know they take cloth with them into the flesh along with the bullet. I thought this

situation was serious, and so I took the two of them to the doctor in my pickup. Several years later, the same fellows floated past me and the one asked if I remembered him—he was the fellow who shot himself. I said I did, and they kept right on floating—happy as if they had good sense."

When Gilmore is not busy with floaters, he occupies his time learning more about the area's history. Gilmore can take interested people to the site of eight small piles of brush which, he says mark the graves of woodhawkers.

According to Gilmore, as members of a steamboat crew navigated upstream past the woodhawkers' cabin, they warned the occupants of the presence of hostile Indians, still resentful of the white man's presence in the 1880s.

On their return downstream, shouts to the cabin brought no response. Upon exploration, the crew discovered the mutilated bodies and gave them the crude burial.

According to Gilmore, the area is loaded with evidence that woodhawks frequently used the area. "There are charcoal fires all over the hills," said Gilmore, "and lots of deer bones in holes around their camps. Old dugouts attest to their residence as do tin cans, brass cartridge cases, and buttons. "They lived a very primitive and spartan existence," Gilmore said.

# Windows Into The Past

They're gone now: the woodhawkers who supplied wood for steam boats along the Missouri, the outlaws who lived in makeshift cabins; the early day homesteaders who stored food in old root cellars—and the women who followed.

An era is gone, but left behind as testimony to past exploits are hundreds of old cabins. Floaters see them virtually every mile of their trip. Areas along the Missouri may have more of these structures than any other in Montana—the area's remoteness has helped preserve them from vandalism. Today, these tumbledown buildings provide windows into the past.

Before the 1900s, Montana had been an extremely sparsely populated area. But between 1897 and 1920 grain prices rose at fantastic rates —faster than farm costs—and the farm population expanded. Helping attract farmers to the area was the Enlarged Homestead Act of 1909, which allowed homestead entry onto 320, rather than 160 acres of the public domain.

Additionally, a subsequent amendment reduced the residence requirement from five to three years and permitted the homesteader to be absent for five months of each year in order to bring in a cash income. The homestead rush was on.

For a number of years all was milk and honey, but following WWI a series of droughts occurred in eastern Montana. Then came the locusts, cutworms, and wire worms. All took their toll, and by the 1930s the area was as devoid of people as it had been a mere decade or two before. All that remained were the luckiest and shrewdest and hundreds of abandoned homesteads.

These shacks and cabins are seen today more than 50 years later in their steadily deteriorating state.

*Left: Robert Gildart photo.*
*Below: Near Fort Union. Jim Romo.*

Left: Jan Mack photo.
Below Left: Abandoned school near Loma. Jim Romo.
Below right: Robert Gildart photo.

*The first cover of LIFE Magazine featured the public works at Fort Peck in a now famous photo by Margaret Bourke-White. Inside part of the cover story was entitled Montana Saturday Nights. Both photos by Margaret Bourke-White, LIFE Magazine © 1936 Time, Inc.*

## DAM HAPPY

When you drive your car along a gigantic embankment in eastern Montana, it is difficult to realize that this enormous hill is Fort Peck dam itself. It is an earth-filled dam—the largest in the world until a few years ago.

To build it, 130 million cubic yards of dirt were removed and 4 million cubic yards of gravel and 1.6 million cubic yards of riprap were laid down. The dam is a hydraulic fill type made by pumping mud and water from four dredging boats through steel pipe-lines to the dam. Today the dam has five power plants which produce a combined total of 165,000 megawatts of power. At full capacity, the lake will store 19 million acre-feet of water, covering an area of 249,000 acres. The maximum depth of the lake is 220 feet. The lake impounds the runoff from approximately 57,500 square miles, a third of the state of Montana.

Behind the dam is the reservoir which extends up the Missouri for 180 miles. With all of its finger-like projections, it has a shoreline equal to the coast of California—well over 1,500 miles long. Even for Montana the lake is big, a condition of which boaters and fishermen are constantly aware. Says one Glasgow resident, "Seventy-mile-an-hour winds that suddenly crop up are nothing unusual. Within minutes they can generate 12-foot-high waves swamping boats in seconds. This is harsh country."

Sam Gilluly, a newspaper editor who spent years covering the construction of the dam, agrees. "Yes, the Missouri is a violent country and it was hard place to scratch out a living. But I really don't remember anyone complaining too much. We were all in the same boat. We had nothing—but that simplified our lives. We were dam happy.

"Construction of the dam was a life saver! It kept me at the newspaper and helped re-establish a better living standard in the Missouri River country. We needed that dam then and I believe we still may."

THE pioneer mother can trek in broken-down Fords as well as in covered wagons. And she can crack her hands in the alkali water of 1936 as quickly as in the alkali water of 1849. When the Fort Peck project opened in 1933 the roads of Montana began to rattle with second-hand cars full of children, chairs, mattresses and tired women. Most of them kept right on rattling toward some other hopeless hope. Some of them parked in the shanty towns around Fort Peck. There, their women passengers got jobs like Mrs. Nelson (*right*) who washes New Deal without running water, or tried their feet at taxi-dancing like the girls on the preceding pages, or made money like Ruby Smith on page 15, or gave birth to children in zero weather in a crowded 8 by 16-foot shack like many an unnamed woman of New Deal and Wheeler. The girl at the bar (*above*) who works as a waitress ("hasher") takes her child to work with her because she can't leave her at home. She sits on the bar while her mother kids with the customers. The group on the right, it will be noticed, resembles a statue recently erected to the Pioneer Mother of the old frontier. No statues are expected at New Deal.

## MONTANA SATURDAY NIGHTS: FINIS

Left: The town of Fort Peck today. Robert Gildart.
Below: The power house, generator and visitor
center. Paul Dix. Robert Gildart. Robert Gildart.

According to Mr. Gilluly, pressure to construct the dam came from the Public Works Lobby, then one of the most powerful lobbies in the country. It organized some of the downstream states into the Missouri River Navigation Association and, together, they approached President Franklin D. Roosevelt. The primary purpose of the dam would be for flood control and navigation.

In October, 1932, without any congressional authorization, FDR allocated $15,000 to a relief fund to begin the massive work project. Within weeks 11,000 men came to the area, threw up shacks, and went to work. Many came with families and, before long, one school teacher found herself in a barracks teaching 352 children in the new town of Wheeler.

To accommodate the influx, the government set up military-type barracks to house the male workers. But most married men could not afford to live in the barracks and house their families separately. They solved the problem by creating the infamous boom towns. Before long a cluster of living quarters cropped up in the form of tar-paper shacks, tents, homemade campers, and holes in the ground. These camps assumed names that glittered in a barren harsh land. Some assumed the hopes of many: Square Deal, New Deal, Park Grove, Delano Heights, and Wheeler.

By far the largest of the boom towns was Wheeler. It featured dance halls and an area referred to as "Happy Hollow."

*Right: Fort Peck generates 165 megawatts of peak power contributing $130,000,000 annually in electricity, most of which is wheeled to the mid-west. Additional benefits are derived from flood control and improved navigation. Paul Dix.*
*Far right: Fort Peck Lake receives more than 700,000 visitors annually. Robert Gildart.*

During the dirty '30s the girls of Happy Hollow and its surroundings generated such intriguing stories that the area drew in many noted personalities from the media. The intrigue of the damsite with its potpourri of mankind beckoned distinguished photographer Margaret Bourke-White who provided Life magazine with its first cover.

Mrs. Bourke-White stopped at Wheeler in 1936 and, as the Life Magazine story goes, demured at entering Happy Hollow. Rather, she asked her husband to conduct an interview for her. While waiting for her husband, a man propositioned Mrs. Bourke-White. She responded by saying that she was waiting for her husband who was inside and would be returning shortly.

"Ma'am," responded the suitor, "you are the most broad-minded woman I have ever met."

Though many prospered by the construction of the dam, one group did not. These were the ranchers, and there is much evidence in the literature to conclude that the government tended to force down prices of condemned ranchlands. "The practice required of the rancher," said the Montana Record Herald, "is that he must make 'offers' to the government officials in charge of buying, starting at the highest figure he thinks is reasonable and coming down in his estimate until he approaches that of the ap-

praised value." The article questioned this method, noting that if the rancher did not like the deal he could "go home and think it over until the river rises, when he can take what the courts say."

Two teachers, Saindon and Sullivan, from Glasgow, Montana, reviewed this literature and published an article in Montana, the Magazine of Western History.

Saindon and Sullivan note that because the land produced good crops of alfalfa seed . . . "many of the landowners in the area have never wanted to sell their property and do not now want to sell.

"It is almost anticlimactic to report," wrote the historians, "that the fiercely independent ranchers and seed and feed growers along the Missouri River bottoms did sell their land and their buildings and moved away. The prices ranged from 82 cents to $45 per acre, which included all buildings and improvements."

But with all of its disregard for the individual, Sam Gilluly believes the dam provided an overall positive force. "It spawned," says Gilluly, "a dozen related projects that were major contracts .in themselves. It helped revive a moribund railway, the Great Northern, that had been in bad shape like all carriers in those depression days. It attracted most of the top journalists and

photographers of the time. Two U.S. Presidents used it as a sounding board for their philosophies when they visited. FDR called Fort Peck national in scope, and he was right. Harry Truman boosted for more power."

But, above all, Fort Peck dam was a salvation for Montana farmers and wage earners. It allowed thousands to stay with the land in this northern section of the state and provided jobs for many other destitute workers throughout the country. It helped cut the relief rolls in every county in Montana.

But the dam was not without catastrophe and Gilluly recorded it. As Sam said, "All hell broke loose on September 22, 1938."

Hinged on the east abutment, a 2,000-foot dirt section of the dam began sliding out into the reservoir. Large cracks began opening up as the great mass of earth started moving. Men ran for their lives, but eight were buried in the slide.

"One man," recalls Gilluly, "thought the slide might cause a quake in Wheeler. Jumping into his pickup, he grabbed his kids and raced out of there so fast the youngsters slid from out of the box of the pickup."

Today, there is little to recall the excitement of this era. All that is left of the shanty towns is a reconstructed Buckhorn Bar. The original burned to the ground in December of 1983.

From the Washington Daily News.

# WILD WEST GOING FULL BLAST IN TOWN NEAR FT. PECK DAM

You have to see the town of Wheeler to believe it.

When you drive thru, you think somebody must have set up hand-painted store fronts on both sides of the road, as background for a wetern movie thriller. But it's real.

Wheeler is today the wildest wild-west town in North America. Except for the autos, it is a genuine throwback to the '80s, to Tombstone and Dodge City and Goldfield.

Wheeler is a slopover from the Government-built city at Ft. Peck dam. It is not on Government property, hence is free to go its own way. These boom towns always mushroom up around a big construction project. There are 13 of them around Ft. Peck.

They are shantytowns proper. They have such names as New Deal and Delano Heights. Their houses are made of boxes like Hoover's famous Bonus Army camp of 1932 on the Anacostia Flats.

All except Wheeler. It is the metropolis of the mushroom villages. It has 3500 people, and real houses and stores. It has 65 little businesses lining either side of the main street. Such places as "Buckhorn Club" and "Rooms—50c" and just "HOTEL."

It has nearly a thousand homes scattered back behind the main drag. It has a half a dozen all-night taverns, and innumerable beer parlors. The taverns open at 8 in the evening and run till 6 in the morning.

At night the streets are a melee of drunken men and painted women, as they are called in books. Gambling, and liquor by the drink, are illegal in Montana. But Wheeler pays no attention. You can sit in a stud game, or keep ordering forty-rod all night.

The taverns don't have floor shows, 'You just drink and dance.' The music goes till long after daylight. You don't have to pay to dance with the girls, but they get a nickel a glass for all the beer and whisky they induce the boys to buy.

Back behind Wheeler is a separate village where the women of easy virtue live. This town has an unprintable name. It has no other name. Everybody calls it by this name. They say a thousand women have heard the call and drifted in for the easy reapings among the dam workers.

* * * * * * * *

Wheeler is two-and-a-half years old. It started with Ft. Peck dam, when some guy brought in a trailer, built bunks in it, and rented them to dam workers at $4 a week.

Ruby Smith was the first real settler. She started an eating place along the road, and within 30 days the town had sprung up around her almost to its present size.

Ruby now runs the Wheeler Inn, one of the biggest all-night hot spots. She goes to bed at daylight and gets up late in the afternoon. She's coining the money.

Joe Frazier is the entrepreneur of Wheeler. Twenty years ago he homesteaded a large batch of practically worthless land and here on the bare Montana knobs. It never did pay its way. Joe Frazier became a barber in Glasgow, 20 miles away.

Then God sent Ruby Smith and the Army Engineers, and they say Joe Frazier will come out of it easily with $100,000. He owns all the land Wheeler is built on.

Wheeler won't exist six months after the dam is finished in 1939. So Joe Frazier doesn't try to sell lots. He just rents them. His income, they say, is $2500 a month.

Wheeler is all wood. There isn't a stone or steel building in town. It has no water system. They have had 16 fires since New Year's. One side of the town has wells. The other side hasn't any. There has been, fortunately, no epidemic.

Prices are typical boom-town prices. Rents aren't bad, but food is high. There is one small wooden church and there are two gospel missions.

Quite a few of the boys indulge in holdups. Motorists on the road, and cashiers behind the cash register, have looked many times down the barrel of a six shooter.

There has been considerable gun waving, but little pulling of the trigger. The thieves take their swag and beat it. Wheeler has not developed any spectacular individual bad man, such as "Curley Bill" of old Tombstone.

And whereas the cowboys used to get drunk and ride down the main street yelling and shooting up the town, nowadays the process is to get drunk and drive down the main highway at 70 miles an hour. They've killed and maimed as many people that way around Wheeler as the tough characters used to with their bullets.

It was the wild criminal driving that finally brought a little law and order to Wheeler. They have a deputy sheriff and two constables now. They don't go to extremes of course, but they pull in the drunken drivers. They say the two justices of the peace have a very good thing.

Wheeler will be gone in three more years. There may never be another one. Somebody had better record it for posterity, before it's too late.

*The Buckhorn Bar burned in 1983 and with it vanished the last remnants of the shanty towns surrounding old Fort Peck. Robert Gildart.*

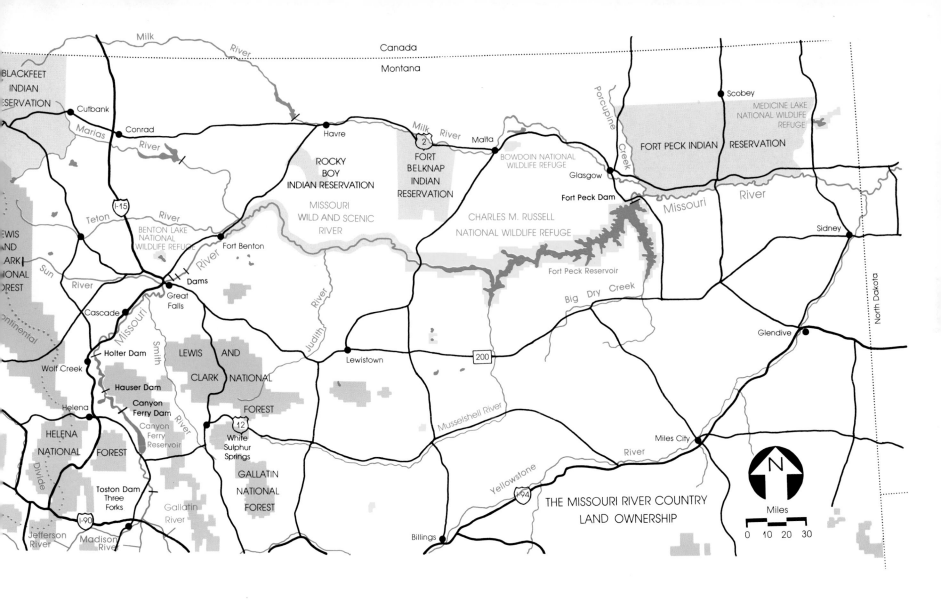

THE MISSOURI RIVER COUNTRY
LAND OWNERSHIP

# The Charles M. Russell Refuge

*Fort Peck and the CMR north of Jordan. Jan Mack.*

About 30 miles east of the Fred Robinson Bridge the Missouri enters the Charles M. Russell National Wildlife Refuge (CMR). The channel through this region, and the one through the next 150 miles, is an old one. The surrounding hills are high and the river has scoured out the surrounding plain to depths over 1,000 feet.

Water flowing from the highlands down to the Missouri has created a forbidden land, grand but austere and exceedingly difficult to roam. For wildlife, the area has been a haven since the first days of recorded history.

In August 1935, Olaus Murie, pioneer wildlife biologist, wrote, "This region as a whole is extremely picturesque. There is a glamour of early exploration over it all, the romance of historical events. The very landscape is appealing. A camp out in the badlands, with the jumble of carved and stratified buttes perhaps mellowed by the setting sun or set off by cloud formations at

dawn, leaves nothing to be desired. In such a setting, the sight of a group of antelope on a ridge or a sharp-tailed grouse whirring from the head of a coulee completes the picture. An occasional prairie dog or burrowing owl are interesting details that belong to the whole. Simplicity on a grand scale is the keynote of this whole outdoor picture."

As the river winds its way through the refuge, it slows and is eventually retarded by the multi-fingered lake created by the Fort Peck Dam. The CMR embraces about 220 of the 297 meandering river miles of the Missouri River Breaks. It is approximately 125 miles long and surrounds Fort Peck Lake. The refuge is the largest continuous piece of ground in the entire Northwest devoted primarily to wildlife, encompassing an area greater than the city of New York and Rhode Island combined. It is the second largest national wildlife refuge in the lower 48 and the eighth

largest in the country. Nearly one-third of the range is covered with stunted forests of ponderosa pine, juniper and Douglas fir. The timber resource has little commercial value but is highly valued for wildlife, soil protection and stabilization, aesthetics, and recreation.

More than 70 million years ago, during the Cretaceous Age, Triceratops and Tyrannosaurus Rex, the largest and best equipped flesh eaters ever to have plodded over the face of the planet, roamed over this same area. The paddlefish of today were associated with the Cretaceous fauna and are typical of that prehistoric setting. More than 90 species of plants, such as Sequoia, surrounded that ancient assemblage. Paleontologists consider the refuge to be one of the most significant pieces of land in the country. Several years ago, "Mort," or Museum of the Rockies

Forty-five kinds of mammals and a profusion of birds and wildflowers inhabit the CMR.
Above: Robert Gildart.
Above right: Pelicans. George Wuerthner.
Right: Pronghorn buck. George Wuerthner.
Far right: Arrowleaf balsam. Robert Gildart.

Triceratops, was excavated from the CMR. Mort graces the halls of the Bozeman, Montana museum.

About 10,000 years ago the refuge was part of the hunting grounds for bands of Indians, lured here by the area's abundant wildlife. Today, buffalo bones lie beneath the base of Pishkins, and archeologists probe the area for clues of early-day man in Montana.

Prior to the dam's construction, the river and area that now encompasses the refuge saw their share of drama. Mountain-man Jedediah Smith camped near the mouth of the Musselshell in 1822; renowned missionary Father DeSmet crossed Big Dry Creek in 1851. The refuge also witnessed the last stand of the Audubon bighorn sheep—killed near Billy Creek in 1916.

Contained within the refuge is the UL Bend Wilderness, which aside from its prairie grandeur, has historical significance as well. In the steamboat era, passengers would disembark and hike a short distance across—perhaps a mile or two—and wait for the boat to make the 10-to 12-mile journey around the U-shaped river bend. After a trip of several months up the Missouri, during which most passengers were concerned about the presence of Indians, the unmolested, wide-open land of the UL Bend provided a welcome respite from both the natives and the cramped quarters of a steamboat.

Today the CMR is much like the UL Bend, a defacto wilderness and a haven for wildlife. More than 40 species of mammals, 200 species of birds, 16 species of amphibians and reptiles, and 17 species of fish occur on the range.

When the CMR was established in 1936, white-tail deer, mule deer, and antelope were the only native big game animals remaining. Since then, bighorn sheep have been introduced and elk have been restocked. Mule deer exceed all other big game in number as well as distribution. White-tail deer frequent the woodlands and agricultural fields of the river bottoms. Antelope occur sparingly throughout the Breaks but prefer the adjacent rolling prairie, especially in the southern parts of Valley and Phillips counties. Numerous scattered prairie-dog towns, occupying over 4,000 acres, have been identified. Such towns are considered essential to the nearly extinct black-footed ferret.

Waterfowl are primarily associated with the Missouri River and adjacent Bureau of Land Management (BLM) lands in the "prairie pothole biome" to the north. The river is used as a resting area by thousands of migrating ducks and geese, but nesting occurs primarily in the "potholes" to the north.

71

# Paddlefish

*Above: The paddlefish, an endangered species, is an anachronism whose numbers have declined alarmingly. The proposed dam near Carter would eliminate much of its spawning area.*
*Below left: The country surrounding Billy Creek is de facto wilderness, though not designated as such. Robert Gildart.*
*Below right: Rocky Mountain sheep have been transplanted to replace the once abundant Audubon Sheep. Ed Wolff.*

Ecologically, the waters within the CMR are prime for paddlefish. At one time, these fish were common throughout much of the Mississippi/Missouri River system. However, during the last 100 years, their numbers have declined considerably. Only six major self-sustaining paddlefish populations remain in the United States today, including the CMR population found in the Missouri and Fort Peck Lake.

A major dam that might interrupt the spawning runs of paddlefish migration has been proposed. It is referred to as the Carter Ferry Dam, and would be located about 15 miles above Fort Benton. If constructed, its downstream effects could be detrimental to this species. The paddlefish is listed officially as a Species of Special Concern—Class "A" in Montana, and is considered "threatened" nationally.

Paddlefish require water temperatures of at least 50°F, moderately high turbidity during the spring runoff period, and suitable substrata for successful spawning. Any change in channel configuration, water temperature, turbidity, and gas saturation as a result of a new impoundment of the Missouri would be of considerable concern.

Prized by fishermen for their large trophy size and also as food, the paddlefish does not bite a baited hook since it is a plankton feeder. It obtains nourishment by swimming along with its mouth open and literally straining its food from the water with its efficient gill-raker system. There is a snagging fishery for this species on the CMR immediately upstream from the Fort Peck Lake.

Paddlefish taken by the snag fishery are larger than reported in any other sport fishery in the country. Females average about 80 pounds; males just under 40. The state record, and possibly the North American sport record, is a 142.5 pounder that was taken in the CMR in 1973.

Paddlefish often live to be 20 years of age, old for fish, and are relatively slow to mature. They spawn over silt-free gravel bars during high spring flows upstream from the refuge. Larval paddlefish have been taken at Coal Banks 156 miles above the reservoir.

Missouri River paddlefish represent one of the last known populations in the nation. The Montana Department of Fish, Wildlife and Parks has requested legislation to allow greater management flexibility to ensure a continuing healthy population.

## Wildlife vs. Cattle

During the winter of 1977-78 more than 4,000 antelope migrated south from Canada to the CMR seeking fuel to rekindle body furnaces that were running low. Many found what they were looking for, but some didn't. Scraping the ground at the refuge, they found nothing but clods of dirt held together by shards of ice. These animals suffered a prolonged death from starvation. Before the death knell finished ringing, 2,000 antelope died, and their carcasses dotted the crusted snow like insects on flypaper.

That was the year after conservationist Ralph Fries was sent to Lewistown to manage the now controversial CMR. He arrived to replace a previous manager who, having watched cattle consume over 62 percent of forage on the CMR, found it increasingly difficult to work harmoniously with ranchers. Fries was thought to be more capable of dealing with hostile ranchers. But after viewing pictures depicting the aftermath of the antelope die-off, Fries was not able to remain silent. His simple public statement stirred the smoldering fires of local anti-environmental sentiment. "The antelope died because there was a shortage of grass."

With the fires rekindled the concerned factions became polarized pitting two threatened species: the individualistic Montana dryland rancher on the Missouri breaks against its wild country and wildlife of inspiring beauty.

In the late '70s, the Department of Interior embarked upon a program designed to reduce the number of cattle grazing on wildlife refuges. On more than a dozen refuges, grazing was eliminated or reduced to levels considered "compatible with the needs of wildlife." Although establishing a policy was not too difficult, implementing it on the CMR was another matter.

For conservationists, any policy that did not eliminate grazing was a setback; for cattlemen and their stock, preservation of grazing rights was a milestone. But the ranchers' elation seem-

*Great blue heron pair with young. Tom Ulrich.*

73

ed incongruous with the very name of the area. What kind of wildlife refuge could give up 62 percent of its forage to cattle?

Later, in Lewistown, Montana, I would learn from Refuge Manager Ralph Fries that cattle on wildlife refuges is nothing new. In fact, on the CMR it has been that way for so long local area residents consider it the norm.

One special interest group has even refused to recognize the refuge's existence. Outspoken, these people refer to themselves as the Fort Peck Game Range Committee and they may represent the most unified of ranching associations.

One of its approximately 150 members is Dave Huston, a man born and reared adjacent to the Missouri River and who has worked there all his life.

Before Dave came along, his father ran a cattle ranch in the area and watched as the land began to deteriorate. Because of the deterioration, the Taylor-Grazing Act was implemented, which limited the number of grazing cattle so the range could recover.

Huston's ranch abuts the CMR. He runs cattle on the refuge using a winter permit which now costs him $3.50 per animal unit month (AUM). He has held this permit since 1947 and for over 30 years has watched the cost escalate from nothing to the point where he believes it is about to go way out of proportion to what the government land is worth.

During a typical winter, Dave will ride every other day into the badlands to feed pellets to cattle. He has six cabins scattered within the area allowed by the permit and out of which he feeds his stock. When the snow becomes too deep, he feeds hay.

As do the other members of the Fort Peck Game Range Committee, Dave believes that the Fish and Wildlife Service wants cattle "plum off the refuge." And, according to Dave, if they do that none of the approximately 150 permitees will be able to survive. Moreover, ranchers believe that if cattle are forced off the CMR more than one million dollars will be withdrawn from the local economy. To them the conflict involves serious business, and although Huston has confused managers with his down-home talk and salty speech, he says ranchers have never won anything with the government. "Only a few stays of execution!"

74

## Governmental Instrusion

In August 1935, Olaus Murie, pioneer wildlife biologist, naturalist and later director and president of The Wilderness Society, was asked by the Bureau of Biological Survey to ". . . size up the wildlife possibilities on the Fort Peck Dam Project lands."

Almost all the land to be included in the refuge had been previously withdrawn from private ownership by the Land Acquisition Section of the Department of Agriculture for the huge Fort Peck Dam Project. Most was unclaimed public land, but about 150,000 acres were owned by approximately 100 private individuals.

As agricultural production declined precipitously through the worst of the 1934-37 drought, thousands of acres and hundreds of homesteads were sold for taxes, abandoned or otherwise returned to the public domain under various government land purchase programs. By the beginning of 1936, most of what was to become the CMR was in federal ownership. But some individuals survived and, as CMR manager Ralph Fries says, "The only ranchers or farmers to survive during the period were the best managers and the most persistent. And those are the people we are contending with today."

Murie spent several weeks during the fall of '35 traveling the Breaks and talking with area ranchers and farmers. He found little opposition to the creation of a wildlife refuge. Some, according to Murie, "begged us to push the refuge idea vigorously."

Grasshoppers had eaten nearly all the vegetation over extensive areas. Cattle must have been hard pressed to find food. Little wonder that his survey showed antelope numbers down. Prairie dog communities were also on the decline; control activities had diminished their numbers with a resultant adverse effect on both burrowing owls and black-footed ferrets.

Sharptail grouse cover was also scarce, though Murie's report estimated that, under improved conditions, the area could sustain populations between 25,000-40,000.

Murie was aware that cattlemen and sheepmen had been promised grazing rights on the game refuge. He was apprehensive about the effect they would have on future range conditions, and suggested that the refuge be grazed very lightly by livestock in sections allocated for elk,

"perhaps on the basis of four cows to the section for eight-months use." Continuing, he said that his suggestion was contingent "on the supposition that we wish to introduce elk into the refuge."

Without a doubt, Murie's report influenced President Franklin Roosevelt's action 17 months later, and so began the problems.

On December 11, 1936, Roosevelt signed an Executive Order establishing the Fort Peck Game Range. Under terms of the order, 980,000 acres of public land were set aside for "the conservation and development of natural wildlife resources and the protection and improvement of public grazing and natural forage resources."

The 1936 Executive Order further stated that "The natural forage resources therein shall be first utilized for the purpose of sustaining in a healthy condition a maximum of 400,000 sharptail grouse, and 1,500 antelope, the primary species, and such nonpredatory secondary species in such numbers as may be necessary to maintain a balanced wildlife population, but in no case shall the consumption of forage by the combined population of the wildlife species be allowed to increase the burden of the range dedicated to the primary species: PROVIDED FURTHER, that all the forage resources within this range or preserve shall be available, except as herein otherwise provided with respect to wildlife, for domestic livestock under rules and regulations promulgated by the Secretary of the Interior under authority of the aforesaid act (the Taylor Grazing Act) of June 28, 1934."

Also contained within the order was a statement that may represent one of the government's greatest of all bureaucratic blunders—it gave jurisdiction of the refuge not to one agency but to two—two agencies with diametrically opposite objectives and philosophies.

Roosevelt's order stated that the two federal departments concerned would have joint management responsibility for the game range. The Bureau of Biological Survey (predecessor of the U.S. Fish and Wildlife Service) within the Department of Agriculture was charged with managing the wildlife resources while the Grazing Service within the Department of Interior was to be responsible for management of livestock

*Opposite page: Don Burke on his ranch surrounded by the CMR. Robert Gildart. Left: CMR biologist examines young Caspian terns. Robert Gildart.*

grazing. To compound the problem, other federal and state agencies claimed a share of interest in the CMR. These included the National Park Service, Bureau of Reclamation; Soil Conservation Service; U.S. Geological Survey; and, in the early years, the Farm Security Administration, and the Montana Department of Fish, Wildlife and Parks.

Beginning shortly after the close of World War II, administration of the CMR was characterized by nearly continuous disagreement and friction between the two federal agencies. Predictably, dual administration did not work.

In 1963, a Public Land Order signed by the Secretary of Interior changed the name of the Fort Peck Game Range to the Charles M. Russell National Wildlife Refuge in honor of Montana's famous cowboy artist. A follow-up memorandum addressed the dual administration problem and attempted to solve the conflict.

"It is my decision that the primary responsibility for policy and program decisions shall be vested in the Fish and Wildlife Service," he wrote. "Control of policy and program by a single agency is essential to properly safeguard and protect the land against devastating erosion and to provide for an increased development of the wildlife resource and the recreational potentials of this region."

Before the CMR was established in 1936, the land had been administered by the Taylor-Grazing Act, an act sometimes referred to as the "Cowboy's Bill of Rights." It required agencies to follow strict procedural guidelines when reducing or revoking grazing privileges. Many ranchers began operating under the provisions of this act. For them, dual administration did not affect their activities as businessmen; they were only concerned when the government changed the grazing rules. When the government attempted to do so, to quote one rancher, "It was like changing decks in the middle of a poker game."

Fencing conflicted with authorized access and pushed the issue into the courts. This problem occurred several years previously when the FWS attempted to construct a fence to prevent cattle from encroaching onto the refuge. In a much contested decision, Judge James Battin of Billings ruled on January 14, 1982, that cattle and wildlife were to have equal priority on the CMR.

In the court's view, the creation of grazing districts withdrew CMR for grazing purposes, and so the courts decided to fall back on the Taylor Grazing Act, which provided the original guidelines under which ranchers had grazing privileges and were to operate.

CMR manager Ralph Fries was directed to roll back the number of cattle grazing on the refuge by one third. This, notes Fries, is an average figure for the entire refuge. Says Ralph, "In some places cuts may be as high as 66 percent; in other places cuts may be virtually nothing. It is unfortunate that our range surveys came out to be precisely one third, but when tallied, that's what our findings totaled."

To help reduce grazing, manager Fries also contemplated "raising the grazing fees to a point where they are compatible with the fair market price."

According to Fries, the fair market value was $8.50. Accordingly, it was his plan to raise the fees until they reached that value. In 1982 they were increased several dollars.

Emphasizes Fries, "We have absolutely no intention of phasing out grazing on the refuge. We just want to see wildlife getting an equal share. At the refuge, cattle had 62 percent of available forage. If you go to a horse ranch, you expect to see more horses than Herefords. If you have a wildlife refuge you expect to see more wildlife than cattle."

And so problems continue on the refuge—different ones for different times. In addition to being directed to roll back the number of cattle grazing on the range, Ralph Fries has been told not to build fences at this time. He was also initially instructed not to implement the "preferred action goals" drawn up in an elaborate Environmental Impact Statement (EIS) that cost the USF&W almost one million dollars to prepare. But, from all indications, he will now be able to implement one of its alternatives.

In summation, the proposed action alternative states that ". . . Wildlife habitat conditions would be substantially enhanced by 2000 with most grazing reductions and other major actions implemented by 1985 and the remainder by 2000. Wildlife habitat management objectives would be met or exceeded refuge-wide by 2000. Significant management actions would include reduction in livestock grazing as well as changing existing livestock seasons of use and modifying existing grazing systems to benefit wildlife. Some soil ripping, shrub planting and construction of exclosures would occur . . . Some boundary fences and a few interior fences would be constructed. Three new reservoirs would be built plus one water pipeline and several troughs. Wildlife habitat would be evaluated periodically to ensure that wildlife objectives were being met; necessary corrections in management would be made. Farming along the Missouri River would be phased out but some lure crop farming would be implemented to decrease elk depredation on private lands . . .

"Federal livestock AUMs (animal unit months) would eventually be reduced 33 percent below levels presently authorized to achieve a light grazing level determined to be consistent with wildlife objectives. Some inholdings would be acquired and ownership of all lands within CMR would be ascertained.

"There would be more opportunities for wildlife recreation due to improvement of habitat and expected increases in wildlife populations."

*Mrs. Myrtle Burke is concerned that her son Don may have to give up his home to the government just as she and her husband did in the '30s. Robert Gildart photos.*

## Three Generations Cope with Uncle Sam

Don Burke lives in one of the most isolated areas of Montana. Once there was a town near his ranch called Faranuf. It took care of ranchers living along the Missouri. But today, the post office and general store are gone. All that is left in the region is the Burke family.

Don, Julie and their two children live about 60 miles south of Glasgow at the end of Willow Creek Road not far from where his folks once lived. Their land abuts the Missouri and is some 30 miles south of the Pines Recreation Area. It is remote in every sense, more isolated now than it was before the mammoth Fort Peck Lake took 249,000 acres of the land.

Don remembers when about 100 people lived along the river. A road was built from Glasgow in 1929 and the Faranuf post office opened its doors the same year to serve the 30 to 40 families in the area. The Lone Pine school, a few miles down the road from the Burkes, had an enrollment of 40 children.

The future looked bright for a bit, then came the drought, an unpredicted plague of grasshoppers, and finally Fort Peck. The post office and school closed. Dust and water—too much of both—forced most people from the land. The government bought up the land, paying in some cases as little as a dollar an acre. Today the ranch once worked by his parents, Junior Myrtle, lays under water. Don, Julie and their two small sons, Keith and Kevin can see it by looking over a bank where his cattle now graze.

Only in 1976 were they connected into rural electric power. A portable generator had served the Burke's needs operating, among other appliances, a 27-year-old propane refrigerator. And several years ago, they received a private line radio telephone from the Rural Radio Telephone System. Before that, the Burkes had relied on a CB base station.

With power and communication concerns out of the way they can now begin devoting more time to the effort of "saving their home."

And they may have to expend a considerable amount. The Burkes have the distinction of being the only private landowners north of the Missouri River within the boundaries of CMR. And that is what worries Don. He owns about 500 head of cattle, and he's concerned that any rules enacted by the Fish and Wildlife Service might hamper his ability to make a living, thus forcing him, his wife and children, off land that's been in the family for 75 years.

Don's grandparents, Jesse and Ruth, came out to Montana in 1909 from Virginia where Jesse had worked in a coal mine; his parents homesteaded in the same area south of Glasgow around 1921. Myrtle suggested the name Faranuf which she still considers to be "pretty natural" as the Burkes are "far enough" from everywhere. Today the Burke children attend the Faranuf school located within a stone's throw of their house.

Retention of grazing privileges seems to be the primary concern of area ranchers, especially Don Burke, whose livelihood depends entirely on his cattle. He's also threatened by hundreds of acres of prairie-dog towns on his land. He can do nothing about these animals because prairie dogs within the wildlife range can't be killed.

Julie Burke, who has the sophistication of a lady stepping out of a Palm Beach condo, is exceedingly comfortable working with her husband. During the haying season she's up with him at the crack of dawn. In calving season, Julie may rise at midnight to help pull a calf. Like her husband, she is concerned about government intervention and their future. She likes seeing her two boys attend Faranuf School and wouldn't want to live anywhere else.

"This is our home," says Kalispell-reared Julie. "It is where we want to raise our children. What right does anyone have to come in and create so much trouble with a family that was here long before the government ever heard of the CMR?"

## Most Remote School in the "Lower 48"

At 8:30 AM each school day, a young woman emerges from a log cabin and walks a short distance to another wood building. At 8:45 she picks up an old bell. The ringing can be heard for over a hundred yards, and moments later, young boys and girls begin emerging from several small nearby buildings. Some belong to the Burkes.

The scene may not be too much different from rural schools around America. But this particular school is unique. It has the distinction of being the most remote school in "the lower 48." Appropriately it is called "The Faranuf School." To the south it is flanked by the "lake," as locals like to call it. To the north it is hemmed in by rolling breaks that gradually taper off into a vast sprawling plain.

The inhabitants of the area consist of only three families: the Burkes, their hired help, and the teacher. Together they have just enough children, five, to qualify for the assistance that was needed to bring in a certified teacher and to receive the aid that was necessary to build an appropriate educational setting for children more than 60 miles from Glasgow, the nearest town.

According to Don and Julie Burke, applications to teach at Faranuf are numerous. "Some people may just need a year of isolation—a year to

themselves to collect their thoughts. And," says Julie with a smile, "they can certainly get that here."

*Schools near Faranuff, below, and the Musselshell River, above, claim to be the most remote in the 48 contiguous states necessitating some unusual transportation to school. Far right: The Musselshell River meanders to the Fort Peck Reservoir. Robert Gildart.*

## Other Problems

Because so many agencies share portions of the Charles M. Russell National Wildlife Refuge, there are many conflicting interests other than the major one concerning wildlife and cattle. Here is a summary:

Recreation: The U.S. Army Corps of Engineers controls Fort Peck Lake and is working jointly with the FWS on recreational development. The corps has expressed interest in marinas, second-home development, loop roads and other intensive development within the refuge, all of which conservationists desire to limit.

Wilderness: Two wilderness areas exist in Eastern Montana. One of these is found on the CMR—the UL Bend Wilderness. In exchange for building a road into the UL Bend, other wilderness areas in western Montana will be established.

Endangered Species: At one time the refuge was home to the black-footed ferret, now on the Endangered Species List. The refuge, according to most conservationists, should serve as an area where they can be reintroduced and thrive. With the negative feelings of many toward the prairie dog, upon which the carnivore is so dependent, reintroduction is difficult. Introducing wolves was also considered by Murie and certain wildlife groups. Today, this is no longer considered feasible.

# Exploring the CMR

On a cold spring day in the CMR with patch snow still lying in the coulees, another photographer and I peered from a blind erected on a knoll and watched one of the most intriguing wildlife spectacles of North America. As the pale sky turned to a rose hue, a group of sharp-tailed grouse began to appear. Where had they come from? A short while ago the broad sweep of the prairie grass seemed devoid of all life; moments later it was teeming with grouse. Gathered here before us, engaged in a timeless ritualistic displly, were somewhere between 60 and 70 birds. Their capers are the most energetic of all the members of the grouse family.

At first these birds began peering at one another. Moments later, a male would suddenly droop his wings until the tips touched the ground. Then, erecting his tail vertically over his back to conspicuously display the white, he would vibrate it sideways so it made a rustling noise. Simultaneously, he erected the neck feathers and inflated the eye combs. Then, with his neck extended forward and downward, the male rushed foward a short distance, stamping his feet and uttering a low-toned call.

Suddenly, the male froze, just as ballerinas might freeze when the music accompanying their superb performance reaches a crescendo. And thus do the grouse remain, poised for a few seconds until their "music" starts again.

Wind is their music, and with another gust of prairie wind, the dancers are off again, leaping high into the air, and fluttering their wings.

Females watch the frenzy of activity from the edge of the "stage." But the dancing excites them, and they join the performers to receive the male of their choice.

There are few places left in America where such activity can be seen, but the CMR is one of them. And so it should be. The refuge was set aside for the preservation of grouse and antelope and an assortment of peripheral species. As a result, if they become familiar with its available tours, visitors to the refuge can see one of the finest displays of wildlife in North America.

The west end of the CMR is the most accessible and offers the greatest opportunity for observing its fauna. A special tour route has been estab-

*Sharptail grouse and courtship display. Alan Carey.*

*Robert Gildart.*

lished at the west end to allow visitors to view the area. The free, 21-mile, self-guided tour leaves Highway 191 just north of Roy. The all-weather road drops down into the bottomland of the Missouri River and passes the Slippery Ann Station, sub-headquarters for the wildlife range.

Along this route, visitors pass nesting islands and platforms of Canadian geese, Indian teepee rings, the King family gravesites, a great blue heron rookery, and scattered prairie dog colonies. Near one of the colonies I photographed a mountain plover and a burrowing owl nest.

Also located in the west end of the range is previously described Rocky Point, once a steamboat landing and a lure for outlaws and vigilantes. Hangings by the law and the lawless frequently occurred in this area.

No off-road travel is permitted on the wildlife refuge, though exploration is encouraged on foot.

The UL Bend Wilderness area is most easily

reached along a series of back country roads by following a map provided by the CMR.

On the east side of the refuge are a number of roads that take one to places like Hell Creek and the steep banks which overlook such historic areas as old Fort Peck.

The most advantageous time of day to view wild animals is in the early morning and late evening. The best seasons are late winter and early spring. But these are also times when following rain, roads have turned to a gelatinous sea of gumbo. At such times, to be safe, it is recommended that visitors check with the regional managers before venturing forth. It is also recommended that those interested in seeing the performance of sharp-tailed grouse contact one of the managers. The thrill of seeing the dance display of these birds is in itself worth a trip into the more remote areas of the Charles M. Russell National Wildlife Refuge.

*Above: Elk calf. Tom Ulrich.*
*Right: Below the Fred Robinson Bridge the river banks sweep outward to become a vast sprawling lake. Robert Gildart.*

# The "Upper Stretch"

*The Missouri begins with the convergence of the Madison, Jefferson and Gallatin Rivers, 2,546 miles above St. Louis. Lawrence Dodge.*

## Three Forks

Several town sites have existed in the Three Forks area, not simultaneously, but as essential predecessors for what one finds today in "headwaters country." To understand better the justifiable pride current residents have for their area, it is necessary to explore the sites that have served as stepping stones in the present town's development.

Gallatin City was the first of these inhabited places. History indicates that it was laid out in 1864 by certain enterprising Missourians who expected the site to become the head of navigation on the Missouri River. They based their optimism on the hopes and dreams regarding navigation which were prevalent between the early 1800s and the time of the Civil War. However, communications were so inadequate that these early entrepreneurs did not realize the existence of a huge obstacle down stream, specifically the Great Falls of the Missouri. Although Gallatin City did flourish for awhile the idea that it would become a thriving navigation port ceased after the Civil War. Nevertheless, it did serve briefly as the seat of Gallatin county.

But after its initial boom, Gallatin City's future did not appear very bright to the sole newspaper of the territory, The Montana Post of Virginia City, or else that older community's jealousy prompted it to belittle the new town.

Regardless, Gallatin City didn't last long. It's imminent demise was recognized as early as March 26, 1876, by Lieut. Bradley. He was enroute with General Gibbon and troops from Fort Shaw to the aid of officers Terry, Custer and Crook in the Big Horn country of his encampment, near Gallatin City and the old fort along the headwaters, he wrote:

"Soon after crossing the ferry (less than a mile below the junction of the Jefferson and Madison and a couple of hundred yards above the mouth of the Gallatin) we passed the few straggling houses known as Gallatin City, and camped on the plain half a mile below. General Gibbon and Lieutenant Jacobs came up soon after we formed camp, returning to the hotel for lodgings after spending some time with us."

Shortly thereafter Gallatin City virtually disappeared as the town of Bozeman began to grow. One newspaper of the time noted that "As Bozeman went up, Gallatin City went down."

Even before the town of Gallatin City had breathed her last gasps, the town of Three Forks, located within miles of old Gallatin City, began establishing her roots. In this case roots assumed the appearance of a toll station for the bridges built in the Three Forks area. These bridges were built in 1864 by James Shedd. On a good day, he collected as much as $500 in toll from the stage coaches, mule, and oxen trains and teams.

Soon a settlement began to grow up around Shedd's bridges. The area became a layover point for passengers on their way to the town of Bozeman. Again, James Shedd was involved, and he constructed his Madison Bridge House, located on the east side of the Madison River. Travelers, according to old clippings, were: "royally received and handsomely regaled by the hospitable host."

If stagecoach business had continued indefinitely, the town of Three Forks, as it officially began to be called in 1882, might never have suffered a slump. But, for decades, it floundered and might have died had not a new mode of transportation appeared. In the later 1800s salvation manifested itself in the form of a railroad magnate.

The tycoon's name was J. Q. Adams, and it was his wish that a new site be established for the town—one that had better drainage and was more suitable for the construction of a railroad. With this goal in mind, a town site was selected, the site of present-day Three Forks.

On September 17, 1908 construction stakes were laid out defining the location of lots that were for sale. Because it was raining, the sale was conducted inside the large Milwaukee freight depot that still stands.

Following the sale, the sound of sawing and hammering could be heard—day and night—for the next few years. By 1909 the town boasted of having 800 residents. Business thrived and continued to do so until the late 1970's when the last railroad chugged through Three Forks.

In 1984 the town appeared quiet but energetic having as one of its major assets an extremely active historical society. According to Mrs. Ruth Buford Meyers, a director in 1984, the society has more than recovered the money expended to publish a history book of the area. The society has also recouped monies used to build and operate one of the more aggressive historical associations in the state.

As with many Montana towns that are young, some of the people living in them represent an earthy group—a group that has dealt with the forces of nature all of their lives and have seen those forces that unpredictably give and take at any time and without warning. The Missouri River represents one of these inviting but sometimes tragic forces. One man has witnessed her capricious nature—or the careless nature of man, depending on the viewpoint.

In a day when we have placed men on the moon, some may believe these river people represent an anachronism and will view those who have dealt with a rawer side of life as quaint. In reality, they should be seen as the people who help us respect humility and keep us in touch with our earthy history.

When I entered the town of Three Forks, Ed Bellach's name cropped up more times than did that of any other person. Edwin Bellach may have pulled more bodies from the Missouri River than any other individual person.

Ed's immaculate though small house with its manicured lawn does not reflect the man's humble beginnings. Bellach was born in a cabin that measured about 20 by 20 feet. The original cabin was made of cottonwood logs. Later additions came from fir logs. But at the time Ed was born the cabin was tiny and consisted soley of cottonwood logs chinked with dirt. Sod covered the roof and once, years after he was born, Ed can remember water trickling down onto the floor weeks after the heavy rains that initiated the leak had ceased.

One night, in the midst of a deluge of unusual proportions, the ridge pole started to creak. "My Dad got scared," recalls Ed, "and he went running outside to get some uncut wood we used to shore up the roof. It stopped the roof from caving in any further. But do you know that roof leaked for weeks after it had totally stopped raining. My god, the sun was even shining. That just shows you how much water this good ol' Missouri River mud can hold."

Mud from his roof and the floor became a part of the river proper, and as far as Ed knows, "It's

*Top: The Historic Sacajawea Inn in Three Forks. Portions of this structure, which was built before 1910, were moved from a hotel built at "Old Three Forks" in 1882.*
*Bottom: Gallatin City, the first settlement near Missouri headwaters is but a ghost today. Tim Church.*

now part of the Louisiana Delta." He quips, "That's how much things have changed around the area."

Just as the mud from Ed's cabin became a part of the river, so has this 74-year old man. Born in 1910, Ed is what many may call a bona fide river rat. People say that he has been doused by the river so many times that if a person were to squeeze him like a sponge, water might gush from his pores. The man has pulled body after body from the river, fished her shores, and more than once has climbed onto her banks or onto the ice after suffering what might otherwise become a personal disaster. When Ed was a youngster he catapulted from the banks of the Missouri right through a hole in the ice. He resurfaced within minutes, more than can be said for the numerous bodies he fished out of the Big Muddy during his various careers in Three Forks.

One of Bellach's first episodes with death along the Missouri involved the disappearance of a man who had been riding a horse. The horse was found right away, but not the body. But the horse did provide a clue as to the body's location.

"It was a pretty good crossing," recalls Ed. "The horse was standing along the bank, waiting, it must be presumed, for its master to return.

When Ed was 15 years old, he almost became a victim himself. Accompanied by a fellow who had an old Model "T" Ford, Ed was fishing for ling. He had set his lines and was on a pair of skates, and had gone over to look at his ling lines when suddenly he slipped and slid down an embankment into some 12 to 14 feet of water. "But," says Ed, "I popped up just like a cork out of the same hole I slid into." Trying to get out, he broke ice almost clear to the bank. Then he ran for the tent that had a blazing fire inside.

Ed recalls the temperature was well below zero and that before he reached the tent his clothes were frozen stiff. He stripped them off and climbed into a sleeping bag. Several hours later he was back out on the bank, catching ling like "it was going out of style."

That was on February the first and ever since that time he's always taken along a cane pole. "Though I've fallen into the Missouri, I've always clung to that pole for dear life. Bend though it might, it's always stayed above the surface, acting like a break against the hole in the ice. Its helped me on many an outing."

Biologists examine rainbow trout in search for clues to its declining population in Canyon Ferry Reservoir. Robert Gildart.

## Trout-Laden Canyon Ferry

In 1982 a cry went up from the thousands of fishermen who had come to expect good to excellent trout fishing from the Canyon Ferry Reservoir section of the Missouri located between Townsend and Helena. The cry of the sportsmen was one of frustration. In previous years, several hours of angling invariably produced numerous large rainbow trout. But utopia had vanished almost overnight, and explanations were being demanded. Why was this most heavily fished section of Montana declining? On a May morning in 1984 Bruce Rehwinkel, a biologist stationed in Whitehall who had been called in to help find probable causes and solutions to the problem, assistant Jim Brammer and I launched a boat near Townsend and began moving toward Canyon Ferry. The boat was specially designed for the purpose of removing fish in a livestate from the river by using a process referred to as electrofishing.

From the sides of our large boat, Bruce suspended wires into the water to which were attached positive and negative electrodes. Between these poles passed an electric current ranging in charge from seven to nine amperes. The fish were momentarily stunned, and Jim Brammer eagerly scooped the inert forms from the murky waters with a ten-foot-long pole.

"Got a big one," hollered Jim back to Bruce in an attempt to be heard over the drone of the generator and boat motor. Bruce smiled back and nodded his head. There are many more fish to be caught but the number accumulating in the holding tank must soon be worked. Bruce banks the boat along the shore and the pair begin processing the fish.

The fish are placed into the solution and, once quieted, are examined to determine their sex, weight, length and, most importantly from Bruce's point of view, their age. Age is one factor

*Mts. Edith and Baldy loom over Canyon Ferry Lake   in the vicinity of Townsend. John Reddy.*

*The Missouri River's reputation as a big-fish river is based on healthy catches such as this one taken below Toston Dam. Robert Gildart.*

that could provide an answer concerning the deteriorating fisheries.

"Canyon Ferry," said Bruce in a reflective manner, "has been known throughout the country as a premiere trout fishery. Not only that, but it is also the most heavily fished body of water in the state of Montana and has consistently yielded catches that would satisfy most any angler. Since 1980, that hasn't been true. In 1983, we made a canyon-wide survey—using electrofishing techniques—and essentially verified what the fishermen have been telling us all along—that fishing is quite poor."

Indeed, something had happened and historical records further corroborated the fact. In other times Canyon Ferry has traditionally provided excellent fishing from the first ice-free days, generally beginning in later March or early April and lasting until early or mid-June. In those times, creel census information indicated that catch rates averaged between one-half and one fish per hour. But during the same period in 1983, fishing deteriorated substantially.

In the summer of 1983, the fishing was also

poor. But Bruce did not believe that was unusual. According to the biologist, fish go deeper and many people are just not prepared for deep-water angling. The anglers' interpretation, however, was that the Montana Department of Fish Wildlife and Parks had stopped stocking fish. But that, according to Rehwinkel was not the case.

"Stocking was never curtailed by the department," says Bruce. "The area has been stocked for the past 16 years with subcatchable fish. The idea is to allow them to grow for a year or two at which time they were generally caught by anglers.

"The recommended plant in Canyon Ferry for a capacity of 300,000 was initially," continues Rehwinkel, "and there is no year the department fell below that figure. In fact, in most years the planting has been considerably higher. Planting, then, wasn't the problem so we looked at other data.

"During the fall run in 1978 we initiated electrofishing from Townsend Bridge down to the Canyon Ferry. During that period we averaged 80 rainbow trout per run that were over 13-inches long. But in 1980, the same technique produced fewer fish. The department didn't react because it was believed that the magnitude of the run into the river was quite likely related to fall flows. Literature is replete with evidence showing that a freshet will bring in large runs. If you don't have one, you don't have the runs.

"But, by 1982, it was realized that the lack of freshets was not the cause of the deteriorating fishing. That year, flow conditions were as good as those in 1978 and still the runs did not materialize. Biologists were averaging below 25 fish per trip. And that," emphasized Bruce, "in conjunction with all the complaints we were receiving indicated our problem was a bit out of the ordinary, and that we would have to try a number of techniques in conjunction with electrofishing."

In 1983, Raywhinkel began a new program. Fish were marked, and from recaptured fish, it was determined that fish caught were actually fish that had been planted that same year. Again, a comparison of these catches with those of 1978—the last year fishing had been excellent—indicated the sampling was only 25 percent of what it should have been. Further, it was discovered that the fisheries were composed almost entirely of age one and age two fish. Because of the short-lived nature of the fish if

something happens to one of these two categories, fishing will be cut in half. But even more drastic, if something happens to both of those two age groups, fishing in the area would be nil.

To some extent, Rehwinkel believes that is what happened.

He knows that in the early summer of both 1981 and 1982, large amounts of water were spilled from Canyon Ferry Reservoir. Dam operators had no choice. Those were years with exceedingly large amounts of rain. Says Rehwinkel, "They had to do something. It was either open the gates and attempt to regulate water flows or let the excess dump all at once. And that action would have played havoc with home owners downstream."

Rehwinkel believes these conditions were the ones primarily responsible for the loss of so many fish from the Canyon Ferry population. The idea seems even more plausible when it is realized the short-lived Arlee strain, the type of rainbow biologists have planted in Canyon Ferry for years, has a natural tendency toward downstream migration.

If so many small fish can be lost as a result of excessive water accumulations, resulting in a virtual depletion of a fish population, the obvious answer is to create a category of rainbow trout that lives longer than just a few years. Presto, as improbable a task as this may seem, the feat had already been accomplished!

In 1977, a strain of rainbow trout known as De Smet were transplanted from De Smet Lake in Wyoming to Harrison Reservoir near Harrison, Montana. They were introduced for four consecutive years to establish a base population. Unlike their close cousins, the Arlee variety, which had been domesticated for 30 years and, subsequently, lost their ability to spawn, the De Smet strain is wild. More importantly they live longer—up to ten years. Rehwinkel believes that adding De Smet rainbows together with the Arlee variety will create more stable fisheries. As a result, biologists planted about a half-million De Smets in the Canyon in 1984 as well as 300,000 of the Arlee strain.

If Rehwinkel's theory is correct, anglers should soon be experiencing catches comparable to those of 1978. What's more, they should should never have to contend with inferior catches again as a new and better strain of fish has been introduced to the Missouri River.

# Lucky Geese

The muddy Missouri has experienced her share of alterations, Some beneficial and some detrimental. One change which became good for geese originated from two groups often though of as adversaries. In this case "reclaimers" and environmentalists conceived a scheme that produced results for wildlife that better than ever existed.

In the late '60s the Bureau of Reclamation (BOR) changed its water management policy to accommodate spring runoffs. To mitigate the effects of excess water the bureau drew down water in the Canyon Ferry Dam area to the extent that the late bottom was soon exposed and turned into a flat of mud.

But, as the years passed, the continuous exposure of the lake bottom to the desiccating spring winds began to alter the mud flats. Another few years and local citizens began speaking of a dust-bowl problem.

In Helena, conditions eventually became so bad that the the Bureau of Reclamation was cited by the Department of Health. Local ranchers were up in arms too. Their farms were being inundated with a fine dirt that clung to crops and penetrated to the deepest recesses of barns and homes. Finally, in the late '60s solutions were sought that would eliminate the problem.

This was a time before the "earth-day" movement. It was a time when the general public was only beginning to acquire an environmental awareness that would bring about the many ecological reforms of the '70s. So the solution was an ingenious one—one without much precedent. It involved the creation of new wildlife habitat from "reclaimed habitat." It further required a large body of water such as only the Big Muddy could produce.

Creation of the new wildlife habitat first involved the construction of a channel that would draw water away from the Missouri, which was used to cover the mud flats. By 1978 a total of four ponds had been completed—held in place by dikes. Then material was dredged from the lake bottom and built into islands.

According to area biologist Jeff Herbert, the joint venture was an advantage as it enabled engineers and biologists to work together to solve

About 200 new goose nests have been created by special dikes and by protecting nest sites. Biologist Jeff Herbert examines one of them. Robert Gildart photos.

both the spring run-off and habitat problems. Working apart, neither would have produced wildlife habitat as well as did the two working together. The end result was the creation from a mud flat of a series of ponds with unequal depths. This variation provided different bottoms which allowed various types of vegetation to establish themselves. In turn, the vegetative mosaic attracted a number of types of insects which then lured a variety of waterfowl to the site, the most conspicuous being the thousands of geese seen there today. But their establishment did not occur overnight.

Historically, geese were confined solely to the lower islands just below the bridge at Townsend near the point where the river flows into Canyon Ferry Lake. This location provided only a sporadic safety for the young goslings on these particular islands as overland access to them was dependent upon the spring water flows. If a low water year occurred, predators had access to the islands. In the proverbial sense, it was either a boom or bust for geese.

Construction of the new islands eliminated the bust and left the boom. Geese began colonizing the small lake islands, and, today, there are over 1,100 goslings, produced by the approximately 200 nests now located on the man-built islands. These discovered later that recaptured fish were actually who once thought 1,000 goslings might represent a hypothetical limit.

Because biologists have easy access to the islands, they are discovering some ancillary facts. Banding studies conducted in the area reveal that geese reared on the Canyon Ferry islands not only return to the region, but, moreover, that they return to precisely the same island on which they were raised.

The area has also attracted species other than geese. A variety of different ducks use the area, but have not colonized as quickly because of nesting requirements. Ducks require more cover which currently is not available. But biologists anticipate that the day will eventually come when there will be more vegetation and with it an increase in the number of duck nests from the

*Shore bird in western glow. Charles Jones.*

1984 level of about 40 to a number that should run in the hundreds.

In time biologist Herbert believes the area may produce appropriate conditions to entice a nesting colony of pelicans. On some of the islands he has found nesting pairs and that, believes Herbert is a start toward the two huge colonies seen in eastern Montana. Those colonies represent two of the 15 remaining colonies of these large birds found in the lower 48 states. Additionally, the area already has between four and five hundred non breeding pelicans in the Canyon Ferry Reservoir area of the Missouri.

But there are problems associated with the new layout that inhibit birds from establishing themselves. When the lake is drawn up to the point where it is higher than water levels within the ponds, water from the lake seeps through the dikes and into the ponds. The result is that water levels are raised within the ponds sometimes flooding over the islands and killing vegetation that is attempting to establish itself.

Another problem with high water is that it erodes the dykes. What is needed is a different type of rock, one that must be imported and that will strengthen the dykes. Because of extensive transportation, the rock would be costly. But it would help with the problem of high water which, in turn, would further benefit wildlife. Eventually as more and more acquatic plants begin to develop much of the problem will be lessened. Plants will help seal the area and help retard the percolation of water into the ponds.

Today, the sound of geese splashing in the water comes from the ponds. Little wonder Jeff Herbert finds himself poking around the area long after the average office worker has retired for the day.

"It's kind of hard to keep me off this area. This project offers an opportunity to watch the progress of wildlife. Each day you can see something different, something happening, particularly in the spring when the willows begin to leaf out and the rushes and sedges begin to emerge. Then, even before the final skiff of ice disappears from the lake, the birds begin to return. And that's one of the most exciting of times."

*Top: The Gates of the Mountains is a rugged chasm that appeared to Lewis and Clark to literally open like gates revealing the mountains behind.*
*Bottom: From within "The Gates." John Reddy photos.*

## The Gates

There are few significant natural features Lewis and Clark missed as they traveled along the Missouri, but the pictographs located below Meriweather Campground near the "Gates of the Mountains" went unnoticed. They also went unnoticed by countless other travelers until Nicholas Hilger discovered them one day in the late 1880s.

Why they went unnoticed is easy to understand; from 1804 until the time of the construction of Holter dam they were located almost 12 feet above the level of the water. The construction of the dam raised water to a point where, today, they can be seen by a person with good eyes from an elevated boat such as the tourboat Scajawea. Their fading images are a legacy of the evolution of today's written word, left behind by members of one of the great tribes that wandered the banks of the Missouri River—and beyond.

"Look at that symbol closely," suggests Tim Crawford as he points toward a small undercut in the face of the nearby cliff. "It is definitely the shape of a buffalo. Look closer and you will see that the buffalo is falling off a buffalo jump. This suggests the presence of a jump in the area, though not a big one. Its not like the big buffalo jumps on the Sun River or the Madison jumps; this was more of a family operation where one person would sit up there waving a stick. He might have a buffalo robe thrown over himself and then move closer. It might take a day or two to get the herd moving where they would be driven down through a notch. Near the notch several people would be positioned in appropriate positions where, suddenly, they would jump up and start waving their arms. That would get the buffalo running down through the notch, and they would follow the Indian dressed in a buffalo robe. The Indian would then jump down onto a small ledge which would further help to keep the buffalo running—running and plummeting to the ground below. The ones in back would push the ones ahead, forcing the entire group to fall."

According to Tim the pictograph panel did, in fact, serve as a form of communication, and, a

*Twenty seven goats were introduced into the Gates of the Mountains in 1951. Today the area claims one of the healthiest populations of goats in the state. Tom Ulrich. Tour boat Sacajawea. Robert Gildart.*

kind of community noteboard. It even had a "locator"—a sign made of a cross and a circle that pointed out to other members of the tribe that a panel was nearby containing information that would want.

In this case the locator directs the reader to the panel which is about 100 yards from the panel wall and about 20 to 30 yards above Mann Gulch, the site of the brutal forest fire which killed a number of men in 1947.

Once the panel had been found, it is thought that the pictures and symbols on the wall would contain some meaning for the Indians. The slashes, for instance, above the buffalo, probably indicated the number of buffalo that might have been killed at one particular time.

Tim also believes one of the drawings may have been a death symbol. Carrying the interpretation even a step further Tim believes that one could take the death symbol and associate that with the buffalo symbol and then assume the juxtaposition to be a historical tale about some warrior who died nearby. But Tim cautions that the interpretation may not be complete. "Its like taking a paragraph, finding three words in the paragraph, and trying to put it back together."

Though Tim Believes the drawings are relative new there is no way of aging them with any real degree of precision. Tim interprets them from an artist's point of view and draws on his degree in Fine Arts to aid him.

"You can tell the pictographs are relatively new," suggests Crawford, "by the way in which the hunter depicted the animal. When a primitive man saw a buffalo he drew four legs because that's what there is. But when a more advanced man—someone with an artistic bent—looks at an animal, he sees something different. He sees a profile and so he shows the animals with only two legs. The pictograph over here might be one of an upside down man, a picture symbolizing death. It could be a warning of some kind, one that advises others that some type of adventure took place. But it could be part imformational and maybe part historical. There are so many different interpretations that no one can say with any degree of certainty precisely what the panel represents."

Tim believes the "medium" was choke cherry and a mineral such as iron oxide that has a purple stain. He further believes the cliff was adorned in much the same manner Indians once decorated the sides of tepee.

Visitors to the area receive information about the pictographs because of the existence of Gates of the Mountains Foundation. The Foundation is publicly owned and leases local sales to Gates of the Mountain Incorporated, a nonprofit organization set up for the preservation of the area. In addition to the dissemination of information, the Foundation's primary mission is to preserve what natural beauty.

"No RV parks down here," emphasizes Tim.

"We try to take people up and down the river and show them the pictographs and other natural history aspects in a manner which does the least amount of damage to the area. No alcoholic beverages are allowed, and it is the Foundation's goal to prevent development. As a result the Foundation has been at odds with companies that have attempted to develop the area."

One company already has purchased an area near American Bar near Gates of the Mountain and is developing and selling homesites. The area is located only 1/4 mile from the wilderness.

Tim says that people who bought property from the American Bar soon joined Gates of the Mountain Boat Club which has the only marina and public access from the local highway. That way they could drive in from Helena, get in their boat, and scoot on over to their homes.

"As soon as we discovered their motive for joining," says Tim, "We asked them to resign from the club. This made it more difficult to get to their lots." Emphasizes Tim, "We just didn't want our area to look like Lower Holter Lake with boats thicker than mosquitoes on a pond. So our boat club numbers are set; we can never have more than 150 and we can never expand the marina itself.

"Gates of the Mountain is one of the few areas into which you can feel comfortable taking kids. Why even a seven-year-old can easily hike the area by camping over for one night."

Left: A much beloved monument to residents of the Helena valley, the Sleeping Giant. John Reddy.

Below: Dan, Bryan and Babe Hilger. Robert Gildart.

## The Hilgers

Slightly north and west of Helena is a large monolith known as the Sleeping Giant. It forms a part of the Big Belt Mountains. Beneath the mountain a ranch can be seen, a ranch that has been woven into the history of this part of the river since 1867.

The Hilger ranch has been in family ownership for more than 100 years, but the last of the Hilgers, two brothers and their sister, Bryan, Dan and Babe, sold the property in 1983. The sale had a proviso that stipulates the land cannot be subdivided and is to be maintained as a working ranch. The sale also provides that the Hilgers, who have no heirs and are themselves getting on in years, will continue during their lifetime to live on the ranch and maintain it.

Throughout the history of their ownership, all members of the family have served as good custodians not only of their own land, but of an adjacent wilderness, The Gates of the Mountains. Moreover, their lives reflect the hardship, despair, hope and endurance required of early pioneer life in Montana.

Initially their father ran a boat concession, but that didn't last long—he was too long going from one point to the other. Jokingly Bryan, Dan and Babe say, "It took our father's steamboat, the Rose of Helena, 14 hours to go down to Great Falls and about 14 days to get back." That was in 1892. He had a steamer built in Iowa and then shipped in two pieces to Townsend by railroad where it was bolted together and then floated downriver to the ranch. The father had hoped to start a commercial business, but the river was too low in the summer. Sometimes the river was so shallow he couldn't even take folks through the canyon. At last he concluded that the Missouri really wasn't navigable above the falls, so he decided to start a commercial tour operation, taking people into the canyon. The commercial trips of today, aboard the Pirogue, and the Sacajawea are an outgrowth of that venture.

One of the most vivid memories Bryan, Babe and Dan have comes not from personal experience, but from one told them over and over by their mother. They recall, she would gather them around the old pot belly stove, particularly on days when the wind blew and snow angled obtusely from out of the sky. Her story was about the day of the great flood, and how she had to scamper for her life with her infant Bryan.

The date of the flood was 1908. It was caused by a rupture in the Hauser Dam. The flood was huge, say the three. It was high enough to take the hurricane lamp off the wall leaving nothing but the bracket. Their mother always chuckled when she related how, after the flood was spent, and all returned home, the violent waters had replaced the lamp shade with a sugar bowl. The bowl was sitting in the bracket that used to hold the lamp.

The dam was made of interlocking steel and reinforced with wooden planking. It broke within hours after a heavy rain began. The Hilger's uncle was digging a well and from the hole could see a wall of water coming right at him. It was about 30 to 40 feet high and brought everything in its path down with it. The uncle quickly hitched a team of horses to a wagon and tried to load up possessions from outside the house. "He didn't quite make it, and four haystacks with chickens," say the kids, "went floating down the river."

In Bryan's words the Hilgers' mother always concluded the tale this way: It seems that up around Beaver Creek there was an old fellow who used to run a ferry boat. On the day of the flood, he'd gone into Helena and gotten himself liquored up. On the way back he decided to stop beneath an old fir tree where he fell asleep. When he awoke, he went home only to find out that his house was washed out. The old fellow said that that was one time drinking saved a life and that he guessed drinkin' couldn't be all bad.

The Hilgers concluded, "Not a person was lost, and only one cow was crippled. Later our folks were able to use some of the planking brought down by the flood to build a barn. The barn is still here.

# Floating The River

Left: Canyon Ferry sunset. Bruce Selyem.

## The Atypical Floater

Albert C. (Doc) Dennis of Campbell, California is not exactly typical of the people who dream of floating the Missouri River. Doc dreams of floating not just the scenic stretches and not just the Montana stretch, but the entire river, from Three Forks to New Orleans.

When I met Doc Campbell along the banks of the Missouri at a campground near the Judith River, he was on his way to New Orleans. He had already floated from Three Forks several hundred miles in his yellow, inflatable rubber raft. This adventurer had braved hail, wind, and snow storms; bucked high waves on Holter Reservoir, fought strong currents with paddle and oar when his small engine gave out in more than just one area, and wrangled rides around 10 different dams. He accomplished all this without extensive plans regarding logistics—just his faith in the kindness of people, and his willingness to pit himself against nature in her various forms.

Doc is not a youthful romanticist either; he's a senior one! Three years previously, when he was 80 and just "a young whippersnapper," the retired dentist hiked the entire length of the Appalachian Trail—from Maine to Georgia.

People doubt his age when he tells them, so he carries a passport, to let them know that, even at the age of 83 (in 1984), he is going to continue to do exciting things. And for him, floating the Missouri was one of the "musts" on his checklist of activities he had to complete.

Many people might believe that if an 83-year-old man can navigate the Missouri, anyone can. To some extent, that is true, but only if you plan with the same detail as did Campbell. Being a retired dentist, the man does things scientifically, and that is how he planned and organized his float. To make the trip, Doc included in his raft a good supply of light dehydrated food and plenty of water. He found he needed almost a gallon of clean water a day, particularly when the hot weather set in and the temperature soared to 109°F.

Campbell also realized his limitations. He knew he would not want to be paddling continuously, particularly against stout winds and across reservoirs. As a result, he equipped his small rubber raft with a five-horse-power engine. Additionally, he included plenty of shear pins. But he still rowed. One June night, caught in Holter Reservoir with snow coming down, his motor conked out and he rowed with all his strength. And the six-foot-three-inch-tall man is strong, as is evident in his handshake. He made it to safety, but it was a miserable night.

Several months after I met Doc, I received a letter from him informing me that he had not quite completed his trip. But he had made it through Montana. Undaunted, he planned to return and start all over again another summer—right where Old Muddy begins at Three Forks, Montana. He said he doesn't mind redoing the entire 500-plus-mile stretch through Montana because, from his studies, that appears to offer the greatest challenge and the most excitement of all that remains along the Missouri River.

## Three Forks to Townsend

To float the same 500-mile stretch that Doc Campbell admires, one begins by launching canoes near Old Gallatin City. Perhaps we'd take advantage of the Montana State Recreation area, camp overnight, and leave the next day. Like Doc, we might even paint a decal on our boat depicting three table forks. Then, depending on our destination, we might want to add a symbol for our termination point.

About mid-way between Three Forks and Canyon Ferry, we encounter Toston Dam. A portage

*Winter envelops Hauser Lake. John Reddy.*

is required, and that is the reason people like Campbell use lightweight dehydrated food rather than canned.

In addition to barring the path of floaters, this dam also blocks the upstream spawning of fish. But below the dam, fishing can be excellent, particularly in the fall. As a result, an autumn Toston-to-Townsend day float is a very popular one—brown trout are spawning, and the fish are concentrated below the dam.

## Townsend to Canyon Ferry

The Canyon Ferry Reservoir area is the one that worried Doc Campbell. It is famous for its sudden, unpredictable storms and Campbell was caught in one in June. At moments, he thought his small craft would be overturned. Through long hours he bailed and fought the wind, attempting to keep the craft headed into it.

## Canyon Ferry to Holter Dam

Floating this area requires several days, but the trip takes one past one of Lewis and Clark's campgrounds and through the Gates of the Mountains Wilderness area. Campgrounds are located in this area as well as trails, the latter of which provide arm-weary rowers a chance to ex-

ercise their legs. Trails exist to accommodate overnight and day hikers. Boaters also may wish to ride one of the two tour boats and take advantage of the informative lectures explaining the geology and human history of the area. Nearby live the Hilgers (see accompanying story), a family well known from the early days of homesteading. They have maintained throughout the years a keen interest in preserving the scenic grandeur of the surrounding wilderness area. As old-time residents, they have marvelous stories to tell, many of which are related at the visitor center adjacent to the marina which berths the two large tour boats.

Once while driving from Helena to Great Falls, I stopped and visited this interesting family. Though reticent by nature, they nevertheless provided me with vignettes of their family's lives over the past century; lives typical of the many settlers who were lured to the West by the enchantment of the "Mighty Mo." What a wonderful threesome, and little wonder they would like to see the area preserved. Here is a locale where boaters and hikers can watch osprey soaring from lofty crags overhead or admire the area's geological oddities. This region of the Missouri River is unique.

## Fort Benton to Fred Robinson Bridge

This is the most inspiring section of the entire Missouri River. Part of its human history, geology, archeology, and paleontology has already been discussed.

Because of the remoteness of the area and the possibility of encountering inclement weather, preparations for floating this stretch should be made to ensure comfort while confronting heat and cold, wind and calm. Adequate water should be taken approximately a gallon per person per day, or one should be prepared to spend a considerable amount of time boiling and filtering water to purify it. Campgrounds exist along the way, and, though they provide outhouses and a few contain shelters from the weather, none provide water. As an extra precaution, some professional guides suggest that floaters have a rattlesnake kit in their possession.

Gear should include hiking boots. Much of the fun is pulling into shore and exploring the various ruins left behind by homesteaders, ranchers, farmers and outlaws. Once this was a wild and woolly area. Outlined below are a number of features that contributed to the grandeur, interest, and intrigue of the Wild and Scenic portion of the Missouri.

*Marias River*—Historically, the Marias River was a site of bloodshed and the forerunner of one of the most significant towns in the West, Fort Benton.

On June 2, 1805, while proceeding upstream, the Marias River stopped Lewis and Clark. Because of exceptionally high water that year on a then free-flowing Marias, a decision was required. Which, they wondered, was the main channel of the Missouri? On the 3rd, Captain Lewis wrote: "...to mistake the stream at this period of the season, with two months of the traveling season having now elapsed, and to ascend such stream...further before we could inform ourselves...and then to be obliged to return and take the other stream would not only

## Holter Dam to Great Falls and Ft. Benton

Fishing is often good through this stretch to Great Falls. Here, the river is broad and slow, until one begins passing through Wolf Creek Canyon. This is a spectacular area, the canyon being composed of black volcanic rock.

Near the town of Ulm, the Smith River enters, a tributary of the Missouri that provides some of the best fishing in the state.

At Great Falls, boaters must leave the river and portage. Though a portage around the falls took Lewis and Clark nearly a month, if you have the same luck Doc Campbell had, it will take you only one day. Campbell found some friendly people at one of the town's parks, and the story of his intentions to float to New Orleans interested them. They drove him to Belt Creek. From there it is about a day's float to Fort Benton.

*Left: Floaters in the White Cliffs area downriver from Fort Benton.   Lawrence Dodge.*

*Bottom: Visitors may expect nightly serenades of coyotes.   Robert Gildart.*

loose us the whole season but would probably so dishearten the party that it might defeat the objective."

Captain Lewis was convinced that the left fork was the Missouri; the rest of the party, however, disagreed. Yet they cheerfully began the construction of an underground cache for the safe-keeping of "articles amounting to about one thousand pounds in weight," to allow investigating the two rivers. Today, as one floats by the Marias, one wonders why there was such confusion. Invariably the river is low and looks like an almost inconspicuous tributary. Where is the free-flowing Marias that Lewis and Clark saw? The answer can be found by venturing up the stream for about 70 miles to Lake Elwell impounded by Tiber Dam. The Marias is no longer free-flowing.

Several days were required for the 1805 expedition to determine the correct source. Captain Clark ascended the Missouri and heard its Great Falls. The falls they knew from Indians was an indication of the major source.

Because of hostile Indians, little more would be heard about the Marias until 1831. That year James Kipp, traveling from Fort Union under the auspices of the American Fur Company, and commanding a party of 75 men, built Fort Piegan near the mouth of the Marias. This fort is considered to have been a forerunner of Fort Benton. Though the fort lasted only a year, Kipp was able to use it as a base for a thriving business with the Indians.

Beginning in 1864, boats withdrawn from the lower river began to appear above Fort Union and enough reached the mouth of the Marias to make it an important location for discharging cargo. This led to an attempt in 1865 to establish the short-lived town of "Ophir."

In recent years, the Marias has provided two authors with book material. A.B. Guthrie, revitalizes Dick Summers from the *Big Sky* and he meets his demise in *Fairland, Fairland*.

The same site provides the setting for Ben Bennett who wrote a historical novel entitled *Death Too, For The-Heavy-Runner*. In 1880, Heavy Runner and his nomadic Piegan Indian band were slaughtered along the Marias by soldiers commanded by Colonel Baker. The author notes that the eastern press denounced Colonel Baker for his actions, although he was exonerated by the Army. The Heavy Runner band consisted primarily of women, children and old braves, and was inflicted with smallpox. Today the incident is known as the Baker Massacre.

*Coal Banks Landing*—Fuel was one of the major problems of the steamboat men and so some effort was made to use the bituminous coal available at this spot. But the efforts proved futile. According to renowned steamboat captain Grant Marsh, "...neither he nor any other of the steamboat men were able to make any use of the native coal deposits." Today, Coal Banks Landing is best known as an access point for floaters.

*Eye of the Needle*—An unusual geological oddity, floaters should not miss seeing this structure.

To reach the "eye" hearty adventurers should unload and remain overnight at their campground on the opposite shore. The next day cross to the far bank and scale a cliff two to three hundred feet high. Though no knowledge of mountain climbing is required, the ascent is best accomplished in a party of two or more.

On one trip to this area, my companions were my son and nephew, each about 12 years old, and my father, who in his later 60s was still in excellent physical condition. The two young boys discovered a well-worn trail through an outcropping of steep rock. At points, the ledges required a boost for both adults and boys.

Upon reaching the top of the cliff one soon finds the eye which has been formed by the process of differential erosion. Below, the Missouri flows quietly, and the height makes its surface appear like glass.

*LaBarge Rock*—This imposing formation was named after Captain Joseph LaBarge, considered by most historians to have been the most capable of all river-boat pilots. Such readily identifiable features were landmarks and mile posts for Missouri travellers.

*Citadel Rock*—As the Corps of Discovery passed this black volcanic intrusion in the sagebrush, Captain Meriwether Lewis, the more descriptive of the two captains, waxed particularly eloquent. He wrote: "The hills and river Clifts which we passed today exhibit a most romantic appearance. The bluffs of the river rise to the hight of from 2 to 300 feet and in most places nearly perpendicular; they are formed of remarkable white sandstone which is sufficiently soft to give way readily to the impression of water; two or three thin horizontal stratas of white freestone, on which the rains or water make no impression; lie imbedded in these clifts of soft stone near the upper part of them;

"...As we passed on it seemed as if those seens of visionary inchantment would never have an end; for here it is nature presents to the traveler a view of vast ranges of walls of tolerable workmanship. So perfect indeed are those walls that I should have thought that nature had attempted here to rival the human art of masonry had I not recollected that she had first began her work. These walls rise to the hight in many places of 100 feet, are perpendicular, with two regular faces and are from one to 12 feet thick, each wall retains the same thickness at top which it possesses at bottom."

Though Captain Lewis spent several pages describing this area he never provided his "seens of visionary inchantment," or this particularly prominent pinnacle with a name. That task was left for later explorers.

*Hole In The Wall*—Colossal statues carved by wind and rain over the years are visible as they rise above the Missouri River below Virgelle. Nearby is the "Hole in the Wall." Though it is the result of differential erosion, one wag has sug-

*Citadel Rock, one of the Missouri's most prominent features, has been a river reference point for a century. Tom Sewell.*

gested that the hole was probably formed by graffiti lovers who literally carved their way through the rock in their eagerness to have their initials remain on a historic site.

Through the years many explorers with a penchant for writing have paused to pen their experiences as they passed through the area.

One historian, John G. Neihardt, described Elbow Rapids, the waters at the base of this great rock, as "deep and safe—much like an exaggerated mill-race." But Lieutenant August V. Kautz, speaking from his experiences aboard the Chippewa wrote: "It is one of the places the little steamboat had to resort to the practice of 'warping' accomplished by putting men ashore to carry a heavy tow-line to a suitable point above the rapids. There it was attached to a "deadman" buried cross-ways on the beach, and the boat was hauled up the rapids by winding in the line with a capstan, or 'steam nigger'."

Today, hikers can reach the "hole" in the wall by embarking on an easy one-mile hike. Though access to the area is unmarked, a well-traveled trail exists which begins at a lone cottonwood tree about one-half mile downstream from the campground. After scrambling through a maze of rocks, one arrives in 30 to 45 minutes at a ridge that overlooks the hole. The "window" is reached by following an easy trail down the east side of the formation and then climbing up a narrow, steep passage.

The hike is well worth the final climb not only for the eye-popping view of the river below but for the close proximity to a number of unique geological formations. As one Missouri River buff says, "Geology here is as current as a newspaper and far more sensational." From this vantage, hikers can actually hear and see erosion as rocks tumble and sand seeps. For the geology buff, there are views of eagle sandstone, joints, and igneous plugs. And wildlife devotees might even catch a glimpse of some of the pack rats which take their caches into small indentations in the rock wall.

*Steamboat Rock*—Floaters who pass a columnar landmark on a bluff north of this meandering river would, according to the Missouri River Commission, be 2,215 miles from the Gulf of Mexico. Knowledge of this distance was a boon to shippers a century ago who were frequently victimized by the readiness of captains to overestimate the freight haul.

*Eye of the Needle. LaBarge Rock is the black feature to the right of the arch. Tim Lucas.*

*Though cattle have displaced many wildlife species, the Missouri country is little changed by man and its wilderness qualities still attract dozens of avian* *species such as the avocet at left. Robert Gildart photos.*

*Cow Island*—Cow Island is in the area Chief Joseph, the Nez Perce Indian Chief, was trying to traverse on his flight to Canada. For ages it was known for its low water as the ideal place to cross the Missouri without too great a risk, providing the U.S. Army was absent. And, on their trek, thus far, the Nez Perce Indians had outsmarted several famous officers. Later, this small band would be revered by some of these same men for their bravery and expertise as military tacticians; but not until after the Nez Perce were subdued by a force many times their size.

Chief Joseph and his band of Nez Perce reached Cow Island and the nearby ford on September 23, 1877. On the same day, before turning downriver, the steamboat Benton had to unload its 450 tons of freight there, as an alternative to Fort Benton, about 100 miles farther upstream. From there, goods would be transported upstream by wagon or a smaller boat. This was common practice, for when the river was low, steamers could not proceed farther.

Twelve soldiers and four civilians were on hand to protect the goods on this September day. There were present with Chief Joseph about 100 warriors. Wisely, the soldiers held their fire as the Indians crossed the river. Even when Indians returned to help themselves to some of the supplies the soldiers were restrained. The soldiers were entrenched at a distance but within rifle range. The Indians kept them under observation.

It was only later in the afternoon that the two groups began firing at one another. Apparently the exchange was brief and no one was killed. For Chief Joseph and his band, the day had been a good one. They were now fortified with food and supplies.

But farther downstream near the mouth of the Mussellshell, Colonel Miles, with a large contingent of troops saw the steamboat Benton. The captain of the boat knew nothing of the army's problems with the Nez Perce and continued his travels downstream. In fact, it was only moments earlier that Miles had chanced upon a group of people descending the Missouri aboard a mackinaw. They had informed him of the confrontation at Cow Island and the escape of the Indians who were now well on their way to Canada. Miles' situation was urgent. He desperately needed the steamer to ferry his troops across the Missouri to halt the fleeing tribe. But the steamer was beyond shouting distance, and the gap was growing with each revolution of the steamer's wheel. Miles' promotion seemed to be slipping beneath eddies of the river.

But Miles, a general officer candidate, was a resourceful man. Swinging his cannon into action, he began firing over the prow of the steamer. Several shots brought the captain to attention and the boat to a stop. Within hours the steamer was transporting troops across the Missouri.

Such is the irony, for if Colonel Miles had been an hour later, or the steamer an hour earlier, Chief Joseph might very well have been able to travel the last few miles he eventually needed to reach Canada—and freedom, rather than defeat near Chinook, Montana.

Blame this outcome of combat on the Missouri, and then visit the battle area to conjure up your own vision of the encounter. Part of the tale is still carved in the banks of the river, and the indentations remain yet for all to see.

*Fred Robinson Bridge to Fort Peck*—Leaving the wild and scenic portion of the Missouri, we float on below the Fred Robinson Bridge to where the river gradually merges with the Fort Peck Reservoir. This section is seldom floated though it is one of the most primitive areas in the country. Wildlife abounds. In recent years a cormorant colony had established itself on an island confined by the Missouri. In the early morning elk cross from one side of the river to the other.

The lake is often buffeted by winds, but fishing for the many different species that inhabit the lake can be rewarding. Paddlefish as heavy as 141 pounds have been taken from near the Slippery Ann Wildlife Station on the Charles M. Russell Wildlife Refuge.

*Below Fort Peck*—The last 125 miles of Montana's Missouri, between Fort Peck and North Dakota, deserves more attention than it receives. It is remote, endowed with an abundance of wildlife, and it is picturesque. Moreover it is the least visited part of the river as upriver portions of the Missouri have received most attention. Because the area is not as well known as the upriver portions, dams proposed for it have a greater chance of being constructed.

# Floating Classroom

Tom Nielson, the leader of Northern Montana College's "Floating Classroom" says he is usually asked each year which of the dozen or so trips was the very best. Invariably his reply is, "The last one."

Tom is referring to his float on the Wild and Scenic stretch of the Missouri. He admires this section and enjoys promoting the educational and physical pleasures derived from an outdoor experience. Nielson has incorporated into a five-day floating classroom, lectures concerning history, science and the art of perfecting outdoor skills.

The floating classroom's staff brings advanced degrees in geology, history, paleontology and technical skills in black powder shooting, cliff scaling and repelling and even rattlesnake cookery.

Students are taught the rudiments of outdoor survival. By the end of the trip, people who had never set a paddle in water before are straining their muscles to conduct with military precision a maneuver whereby each party in the rear attempts to weave in and out of the line of canoes preceeding it.

Lectures bring to life the skirmish of the Nez Perce at Cow Island, Lewis and Clark, and Camp Cooke with its amazing Sarah Canfield.

You might find yourself rising well before sunrise, binoculars in hand, to enjoy the sight of a poorwill breaking from its evening torpor.

And you can float the mighty Missouri River—watching pelicans soar overhead, surprising a fawn coming down for water, feeling the tug of the current drawing you downstream.

To be a part of it, all you need do is sign up—for one of the 20 spots open in the class each summer.

*Robert Gildart photo.*

The floating classroom is:
Part survival training.
Part geology—this igneous instrusion is an example of the kind of phenomenon that is explained
Part history—Dr. Harrison Lane of Northern Montana College, Havre illuminates the Missouri Country's past.
Part recreation—Tom Nielson gives the crew advice on how to keep a trim ship.
Robert Gildart photos.

# Epilogue

## HERITAGE LOST, HERITAGE GAINED

In 1833 the staid, scientifically minded Prince Alexander Philip Maximilian of Wied-Neuwied traveled through what is now the wild and scenic portion of Montana's Missouri River. Normally reticent by nature, he was prompted to write in glowing terms about the area.

". . . on this day," wrote the nobleman, "it had been very warm, but the evening was rather cool. The people laid aside their oars, and suffered the boat to drift down the stream. A solemn silence prevailed in the vast solitary wilderness, where Nature, in all her savage grandeur, reigned supreme. Not a breath of air was stirring, buffaloes were quietly grazing on the sides of the hills, and even my bears lay still . . .; nobody spoke a word; it seemed as if we were involuntarily led by the impressions made by the scene, at the solemn evening hour, to give way to serious contemplation, for which there was ample matter."

Today 11 million persons live in the six states through which the Missouri flows. Dams have been constructed along this river and vastly alter the pristine state of nature. By 1983, in Montana alone, 10 dams had been constructed along the Missouri. These included: the diversion dam at Toston, Canyon Ferry, Hauser, Holter, Black Eagle, Morony, Ryan, Cochrane, Great Falls and Fort Peck. More are proposed. The backwaters of six gigantic dams virtually lap onto the walls of the next dam upstream. Beneath these structures are buried dozens of historic sites, early forts, ancient Indian villages and religious shrines.

Over the years, development of the Missouri has been advocated by both the Army Corps of Engineers and the Bureau of Reclamation. Fort Peck Dam in eastern Montana was constructed by the corps to store water and maintain a barge canal on the lower Missouri. Historically, the corps, favoring downstream protection, proposed what was known as the Pick Plan for flood control and navigation. The bureau, favoring upstream users, pushed the Sloan Plan for irrigation and hydroelectric power. The two agencies fought bitterly over their respective plans. When President Franklin D. Roosevelt advocated creation of a third water-development agency, the Missouri Valley Authority, officials of the two rival agencies met to resolve their disagreement. After a two-day meeting, the bureau and the corps announced that they would combine the plans and build all the dams! Thus was born the disastrous Pick-Sloan Plan of 1944 which authorized more than 100 dams in the Missouri's watershed at a cost exceeding $6 billion. At the time an editorial in the St. Louis Post-Dispatch denounced the Pick-Sloan Plan as a "loveless, shameless, shotgun marriage of convenience." According to many, the hodgepodge water projects indeed represented not a "plan" at all, but a wasteful and destructive misuse of the river's resources and a mockery of rational development.

Today, as we look at the rapid commercially directed development of the Missouri's natural resources, we see not only heritage lost but also that which has been preserved. Even if—as some claim—the developments along the Missouri are symbols of the waste of our earlier natural resources, part of the river also reflects our nation's latter-day conservation ethic. Here, wildlife is still abundant, including mule deer, white-tail deer and antelope. Elk and bighorn sheep have been reintroduced into portions bordering the wild Missouri. And there are sections where a person can float undisturbed, watching time slip by and never sense a loss.

As Ken Walcheck, a biologist with the Montana Department of Fish Wildlife and Parks tells the story, salvation of the river was due to the efforts of a number of people. The time was 1971, and the setting the Cascade County Courthouse. A bill had been introduced by Congress, which proposed setting aside the last remaining free-flowing vestige of the Missouri as a Wild and Scenic River. People who were to testify on behalf of the river had come from near and far. Ken likes these people and enjoys telling about the activities of conservation friends who made special efforts to reach the courthouse. Don Aldrich, president and spokesman for the Montana Wildlife Federation, left his vacation campsite in the Bitterroot Mountains, hiked four hours and drove eight more to present the federation's position. Lou Hagener, professor of botany at Northern Montana College in Havre, left his plant collecting site during a downpour in the Bear Paw Mountains and fought both clock and steering wheel as he drove over backcountry roads that had turned into sticky gumbo.

What they had to say is now history, but some of the speeches are worth repeating, for the Missouri is never safe, as one of the following excerpts indicates.

Clifton R. Merritt for The Wilderness Society: ". . . Most of the land involved is already in public ownership . . . . Perhaps nowhere else in the United States would it be possible to prepare so well for tomorrow's wildlife resources as in the Missouri Breaks . . . In short, this magnificent river segment is rich beyond measure in scenic, recreational, wildlife, historical, archeological, and geological values . . . Strange as it may seem, a wild river has become a rare resource in Montana. It is an even more scarce natural asset elsewhere in the United States. It is priceless to the nation. Surely, this country can afford to set aside 7 percent of the mighty Missouri as a living memorial to the intrepid Lewis and Clark expedition."

John J. Craighead of the Montana Cooperative Wildlife Research Unit: ". . . the economic assets claimed by the dam proponents, can also be claimed by the preservationists. And in this regard we should keep in mind that a dam is mortal with an economic lifespan of perhaps 50 years; a free-flowing Missouri is immortal and the economic benefits tend to compound and they will last as long as our people respect their history, love the land and water and seek natural beauty."

Dr. Louis W. Hagener, Professor of Biology Northern Montana College: "From an educational standpoint, the river is invaluable to us. The history of it is important—as is its archeology, geology, and biology."

Mrs. Patricia Antonick, private citizen and Montana native: "... Charlie Russell left us a painting, done in 1900, entitled, 'Before the White Man Came.' A gift of ours for future generations should be a free-flowing stretch of the mighty Missouri as it was before the developers came."

Mr. William A. Spoja, citizen of Lewistown: "...the following representation is made in behalf of the Missouri River Development Association, the Lewistown Chamber of Commerce...and the Lewistown Boat Club...

"It is not the way of central Montana's people to permit a few willful, selfish persons to turn their home into a wasteland to serve as someone else's playground... The proposed Missouri Breaks Scenic Recreation River would do grievous and lasting harm to the people in the eight counties adjacent to it...Thoughtful citizens recognize it for the fool's gold that it is...Our young people have left in hordes because they couldn't find jobs. They must go elsewhere to make a living. Older people, too, have left...We need new development, new opportunities for our people... The Missouri River can be the great source for the new wealth and development that we must have in the eastern congressional district of Montana.

"Senate bill 1450 would kill these developing possiblities and ... prevent, perhaps forevermore, the development of the power, navigation irrigation, recreation, and other possibilities that are so important to all of us."

And so we move on into the future, drifting with the flow, knowing that some of the heritage of the Missouri has been lost and some preserved, and realizing that the river's contour will never remain static.

*Robert Gildart photo.*

You can never put your hand into the river in the same place twice.
Heraclitus.

*At Hole in the Wall. Robert Gildart.*

## Next in the Montana Geographic Series

### Exploring Montana with the Pioneer Naturalists

From Lewis and Clark to Teddy Roosevelt, the most detailed accounts of Montana before the coming of development were left by explorers with a deep curiosity about the animals and plants of this largely unknown land. No single history of Montana has fully captured the colorful exploits and sharp observations of those who came to explore and to record its natural history. There were the European men of leisure to whom coming of age meant adventures in the wilderness. There were the famous–David Thompson and John James Audubon. There were the pious such as Father Desmet, and there were the route scouts and hunters with the railroad surveys. After a century of largely amateur naturalists, finally there were the professional scientists such as the University of Montana's Morton Elrod. Taken together, these accounts paint a panorama of Montana before settlement and chronicle its changing character in the 19th century. By Larry Thompson.

### Montana's Indians Yesterday and Today

Books abound on Montana's Indians in the past, but this is the first book to combine a colorful, accurate, concise history of the Indians that occupied what is now Montana and also to review the lifestyle, resource base, leadership and aspirations of Montana's Indians today. By William Bryan with photography by Michael Crummett.

**Other Titles in Planning and Production**
**The Yellowstone River——by Bill Schneider**
**The Continental Divide——by Bill Cunningham**
**Eastern Montana's Mountain Ranges——Mark Meloy**

# MONTANA MAGAZINE
## Tells The Whole Montana Story

The history, the wild back country, the people, the wildlife, the towns, the lifestyles, the travel — these things are Montana — unique among the states. Montana Magazine brings you the Montana story six times a year in a beautiful, long-lasting magazine.
Its hallmark is full-page color photography of Montana from the peaks to the prairies.

### REGULARLY FEATURED DEPARTMENTS:

WEATHER
GEOLOGY
HUNTING
  AND FISHING
OUTDOOR
  RECREATION
HUMOR
PERSONALITY
GARDENING
DINING OUT

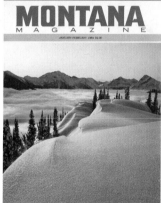

## Montana Magazine Because You Are A Montanan

For subscription information write:
**MONTANA MAGAZINE**
Box 5630
Helena, MT 59604

**Front Cover Photos:**

The Missouri River near Fort Benton, Paul Dix.
Rancher Don Burke and son on the Charles M. Russell Refuge. Robert Gildart
The Eye of the Needle. Robert Gildart
Pelicans near Cascade. Robert Gildart
Prickly Pear. Robert Gildart